SEXUAL ASPECTS OF
CARDIOVASCULAR DISEASE

Sexual Medicine, Volume 10
HAROLD I. LIEF, M.D., SERIES EDITOR

SEXUAL ASPECTS OF CARDIOVASCULAR DISEASE

Chris Papadopoulos, M.D.

New York
Westport, Connecticut
London

Library of Congress Cataloging-in-Publication Data

Sexual aspects of cardiovascular disease / Chris Papadopoulos.
          p.   cm. — (Sexual medicine ; v. 10)
          Includes bibliographies and index.
          ISBN 0-275-92523-4 (alk. paper)
          1. Cardiovascular system—Diseases—Patients—Sexual behavior.
     I. Papadopoulos, Chris. II. Series.
          [DNLM: 1. Cardiovascular Diseases—physiopathology.
     2. Cardiovascular Diseases—psychology. 3. Cardiovascular Diseases—
     rehabilitation. 4. Sex. 5. Sex Behavior. W1 SE99F v.10 / WG 100
     S518]
     RC669.S49   1989
     616.1071—dc20   89-3973

Library of Congress Catalog Card Number: 89-3973
ISBN: 0-275-92523-4

First published in 1989

Praeger Publishers, One Madison Avenue, New York, NY 10010
A division of Greenwood Press, Inc.

Printed in the United States of America

∞

The paper used in this book complies with the Permanent
Paper Standard issued by the National Information Standards
Organization (Z39.48--1984).

10 9 8 7 6 5 4 3 2 1

To

those who care for the cardiovascular patient

Contents

Preface

The comprehensive approach to the care of patients with chronic cardiovascular illness involves alleviation of their symptoms and enhancement of their functional status, as well as improvement of the outcomes of acute episodic complications.

With the increasing recognition that sexual function is an important contributor to the quality of life of many patients with cardiovascular disease, the relationships of the illness to sexual function are more often addressed by physicians in counseling their patients. Cardiac patients, as well as their spouses, are also more likely to query their physicians about resumption of sexual activity following an acute coronary episode such as myocardial infarction or coronary bypass surgery because this aspect of recovery has been popularized in the public — and patient — educational literature.

As noted by Dr. Papadopoulos, despite these advances information about sexual function or dysfunction is absent or limited in the data reported from most clinical trials of cardiovascular diseases and therapy. Further, myths and misinformation about sexual function following a coronary event abound, and health professionals are often unaware of relevant substantive data. Unfortunately, elderly patients in general are also rarely queried or counseled about sexual function. The interaction of the patient's psychological state with sexual concerns and problems is often not appreciated, although psychologic problems are recognized as concomitants of many cardiac illnesses. This well-referenced volume is all the more valuable as a resource for clinicians in that the author has long been a recognized contributor to the information base about sexual aspects of cardiovascular disease.

Appropriately highlighted is that a sexual history is part of the comprehensive information needed about all patients, and that the impact of the illness and of related pharmacotherapy and/or surgery on sexual functioning must be assessed. The scope of information to be gathered and the techniques for so doing are presented, with suggestions on the content of and the methods for sexual counseling of the spouse as well as the patient with cardiovascular disease.

Although sexual aspects of coronary disease have received predominant attention in professional and lay publications, sexual function is often influenced by other cardiovascular problems and their therapies. Particularly in the patient with hypertension, the disease, its pharmacotherapy, and its complications (including stroke and renal failure) may all adversely affect sexual function. Specific inquiry about sexual function is requisite when addressing the side effects of antihypertensive therapy, but it is noted that most available data are derived from studies involving predominantly young and middle-aged men. An excellent chapter summarizes the interrelationships of sexual function and a variety of cardiovascular and other drugs.

Non-coronary heart diseases, particularly congenital heart disease and valvular heart disease (as well as corrective surgery for these problems) entail concerns not only for subsequent sexual function but for the safety and desirability of pregnancy. Sexuality and the concerns about childbearing for heart transplant patients are also addressed.

The pathophysiologic basis for sexual dysfunction in patients with aorto-iliac occlusive disease and in those following cerebrovascular accident is reviewed, with presentation of the surgical interventions, rehabilitation, and counseling that are likely to optimize the restoration of sexual function.

Counseling of the patient and spouse regarding sexuality and sexual function is a component of comprehensive cardiac care. The resources available in this monograph should enhance the clinician's knowledge, ability, and confidence in providing guidance in this important aspect of recovery.

Nanette K. Wenger, M.D.
Professor of Medicine (Cardiology)
Emory University School of Medicine
Director, Cardiac Clinics
Grady Memorial Hospital

Foreword

The number of people with cardiovascular disease is huge. The statistics are staggering. In the United States alone, there are 60 million people with hypertension; 160,000 die of stroke each year; those stroke victims who live join a pool of 2 million stroke survivors; 200,000 people have coronary artery bypass grafts (CABG) each year; 100,000 cardiac pacemakers are inserted annually; 1.5 million people each year have a myocardial infarction. The lives of survivors are often profoundly affected by their illnesses and treatments.

It is only in the last decade or two that most physicians are giving serious attention to the quality of life of the many people with cardiovascular illness. The emphasis has always been on survival rather than the kind of life a person might lead after being afflicted with heart or vascular disease. As more and more people survive because of modern technology, such as CABGs, cardiac pacemakers, and improved techniques of vascular surgery, the attention of the health professional inevitably has shifted to quality of life issues.

Quality of life can be defined in much the same terms that Freud used to define mental health, namely the capacity for work and for love. The ability of patients to return to work, or at least to productive and creative use of recreational or retirement time, and the capacity for a close intimate relationship are the major ways in which one can gauge the quality of life. While intimacy can be achieved without good sexual relationships, it doesn't happen all that often. For most people, satisfactory sex is a necessary part of intimacy. Cardiovascular disease threatens sexual function. For example, after a myocardial infarction, approximately 25 percent stop having sex altogether, and about 50 percent have less sex. Only in one in four is sex unaffected. A very tiny percent increase frequency presumably because they use sex to draw closer to one another, to gain reassurance that life is still very much worthwhile. Sexual adaptation is also threatened by open heart surgery although frequently the preoperative medical condition had been so bad and, as a consequence, sexual function had been so poor that the increased cardiac function has a beneficial effect on sex. Frequently after an MI or cardiac surgery the spouse has more anxiety than the patient, including a fear of coital death. (Throughout the book the author pays very special attention to the spouse's concerns and reactions.)

To complicate matters, even when the illness itself affects sexual functioning (for example, hypertension alone causes impotence in approximately 17 percent of men), the problem is compounded by the use of cardiovascular drugs, many of which have adverse sexual side effects.

In this very welcome addition to the series on "Sexual Medicine," Chris Papadopoulos, Chief of Cardiology, Harbor Hospital Center, Baltimore, takes the reader through the various types of cardiovascular diseases with separate chapters on coronary artery disease, the non-coronary cardiac patient (for example, valvular disease), the quality of life and sexual activity after cardiac surgery, and sexual function associated with aorto-iliac occlusive disease and surgery. In a chapter on cardio-vascular drugs, he describes each drug and its effects on sexual desire, erection and ejaculation, as well as some dimensions of female sexuality, and has developed a useful chart summarizing this data. His final chapter on sexual counseling and rehabilitation summarizes his recommendations for the clinician and other health professionals.

Papadopoulos believes that physicians have still not learned to address these issues properly. In a study he himself conducted, he found that in the early part of the 1970s, only 11 percent of physicians initiated discussion of sexuality with MI patients prior to discharge. At the end of the decade, this had increased to 18 percent. It is doubtful whether this percentage has increased a great deal in subsequent years. This is how Papadopoulos expresses it: "Sexual concerns and anxiety should be addressed early and sexual counseling should be part of early rehabilitation, starting before and continuing after discharge from the hospital. The patient has to adapt emotionally to his handicap, and the family must be prepared for adaptation. A sympathetic and attentive physician or nurse may help the patient express his or her concerns and alleviate any fears. No health professional should assume that every person, who has suffered a physical impairment, would have withdrawn his emotional attention from ordinary interests and his sexuality."

Sexual adaptation is one of the important facets of the ways in which a person adapts to stress, particularly to illness. Psychological consequences of illness often add to the patient's stress. Some degree of anxiety and depression are commonplace, and people with cardiovascular illness, even if they have not had a myocardial infarction or cardiovascular surgery, experience those ·feelings. Depression may bring with it feelings of worthlessness, guilt, helplessness, hopelessness, sadness, and loss of interest in work and in sexual activity. The wise and humane health professional will pay particular attention to these aspects of rehabilitation.

This volume will be very useful to physicians, nurses, social workers, and other health professionals who take care of the millions of people with these illnesses.

Harold I. Lief, M.D.
Professor Emeritus of Psychiatry
University of Pennsylvania
School of Medicine

SEXUAL ASPECTS OF
CARDIOVASCULAR DISEASE

1
Coronary Artery Disease and Sexuality

In the United States alone, more than 900,000 people yearly survive the epidemic of myocardial infarction (American Heart Association 1988). For many years the rehabilitation of these patients mainly involved their return to the optimal physical and vocational status. Successful rehabilitation, however, should include consideration of their sexual activity. Sex is woven into the everyday life of many patients. High percentages of patients who suffer a myocardial infarction are sexually active prior to the occurrence of this event (Bloch et al. 1975; Horgan and Craig 1978; Papadopoulos 1978). Concerns and myths about resumption of sexual activity are abundant and are often accentuated by the press and television and, unfortunately, at times by medical professionals.

In the last two decades several studies addressed the topic of sexual activity after myocardial infarction. These studies dealt with from 39 to 150 patients, who were mostly male. A few of the studies included small numbers of female patients and only one (Papadopoulos et al. 1983) exclusively studied a group of female patients. The mean age of the patients in practically all of the reports was the early fifties. These studies varied in the method of interviewing the patients and in the topics that were addressed. It was obvious, however, that myocardial infarction had a negative impact on the sexual activity of the patients who were sexually active before the event. From 10 to 44 percent of the patients, as noted in Table 1, do not resume sexual activity, while 20 to 77 percent resume it with reduced frequency. In our studies based on female patients (Papadopoulos et al. 1983), on male patients (Papadopoulos 1978), and on interviews with wives of myocardial infarction patients (Papadopoulos et al. 1980) approximately one-quarter of the patients did not resume sexual activity (27 percent, 21 percent, and 24 percent, respectively), one-quarter did not change the frequency of sexual activity (27 percent, 25 percent, and 22 percent) and half decreased the sexual activity (44 percent, 54 percent, and 49 percent). Only in a few studies, small numbers of patients increased sexual activity after myocardial infarction (1 to 12 percent). Among male patients the frequency of impotence was 1 to 49 percent (Table 1). Variation in the numbers could be due to the fact that some studies included patients with partial or intermittent impotence.

Responses described for no resumption of sexual activity have been loss of libido, the patient's or the partner's fears of risk in resuming sexual relations, the patient's or the spouse's excuse to stop sexual relations that were not enjoyable

TABLE 1
Studies of the Sexual Activity after Myocardial Infarction

Author	Number of patients (women)		Mean age	Did not resume SA	Post MI frequency of SA			Impotence	Symptoms with SA
					same	increased	decreased		
Tuttle et al. (1964)	39	(0)	50±	10%	30%		60%	10%	
Hellerstein and Friedman (1970)	48	(0)	53		42%		58%	0%	42%
Bloch et al. (1975)	100	(12)	58	22%	25%	2%	51%	1%	
Amsterdam et al. (1977)	107	(0)	53		53%	4%	43%	49%	
Datey (1977)	125	(0)	46	23%			77%		16%
Kavanagh and Shephard (1977)	161	(0)	51		50%		50%		
Stern et al. (1977)	68	(13)	53	9%		10%	20%		
Horgan and Craig (1977)	100	(14)	57	34%			57%	15%	
Papadopoulos (1978)	135	(17)	56	21%	25%		54%	10%	51%
Mehta and Krop (1979)	100	(0)	59	30%		12%	59%	45%	
Mann et al. (1981)	88	(9)	54	19%		5%	68%	8%	8%
Grand et al. (1982)	120	(12)	54	10%	38%	1%	61%	40%	>9%
Gupta and Singh (1982)	150	(0)	35–76						26%
Sjogren and Fugl-Myer (1983)	49	(0)	56				63%	45%	>37%
Papadopoulos et al. (1983)	130	(130)	54	27%	27%	1%	44%	N/A	57%

before the myocardial infarction, persistence of the patient's cardiac symptoms, the patient's impotence, lack of available partner, or the patient's depression. One patient of ours would not resume sexual activity because he heard of someone "who died during sex after a heart attack." Another said that she "had always been frigid and having a heart attack gave her a good reason to stop sexual activity." Yet another stated that her husband "used her heart attack as an excuse to quit sexual relations because he had had sexual problems for about a year." Similar reasons were offered by patients for resuming sexual activity with decreased frequency.

The patient's age and that of the partner, the previous level of sexual activity, and the discussion of sexual relations between the couple are positive factors in resuming sexual activity (Papadopoulos et al. 1980; Papadopoulos et al. 1983). Among the patients who resume sexual activity, there is often a change in technique or positions, mainly avoidance of variety. They restrict themselves to the basic and most comfortable positions previously used (Papadopoulos et al. 1980; Papadopoulos et al. 1983). Often the patients do not eliminate the standard "missionary position." In another study, most patients had no change in patterns of foreplay or the position adopted during coitus and of those that reported a change, most had adopted a more passive position (Kavanagh and Shepherd 1977).

The frequency of sexual activity may be decreased by 25 to 75 percent (Tuttle et al. 1964; Hellerstein and Friedman 1970; Papadopoulos et al. 1983). In addition to a decrease in frequency, a decline in the quality of sexual activity is often seen in patients with myocardial infarction (Wishnie, Hackett and Cassem 1971; Hellerstein and Friedman 1970; Papadopoulos et al. 1983). The time of resumption also varies tremendously. In one of our studies, the time varied from 2 weeks to 12 months (Papadopoulos 1978). The average in that study was 10.7 weeks. Lower average time of resumption was reported in more recent studies, 9 weeks (Mann, Yates and Raftery 1981) and 8.5 weeks (Papadopoulos et al. 1983). Fear, depression, and symptoms of coronary artery disease may delay the time of resumption of sexual activity.

Impotence and other sexual difficulties were reported in a study designed to investigate the long-term effects of myocardial infarction on marital and sexual functioning (Mehta and Krop 1979). Thirty-seven percent of patients had premature ejaculation, 54 percent manifested retarded ejaculation, and 60 percent had erectile difficulties at least half of the time.

The patients may report cardiac symptoms with sexual activity, but the frequency has varied in various reports. This is probably due to the wide ranging number of patients in the various studies, the fact that some studies included patients from exercise rehabilitation programs, and the fact that some reported only the symptoms of angina, while others included other cardiac symptoms (shortness of breath, fatigue, sweating, and palpitations). The incidence of symptomatology varied from 8 to 57 percent. Symptoms can occur during all phases of sexual activity but may be more frequent and marked during the resolution phase (Gupta and Singh 1982). In our studies (Papadopoulos 1978; Papadopoulos et al. 1983) the incidence of chest pain was much higher among females (52 vs. 9.2 percent). It is conceivable that this represents more awareness of the symptoms during intercourse by the female patient or less participation in exercise programs. It is, however, compatible with the observation that women in general have a higher incidence of angina after myocardial infarction (Tofler et al. 1987).

Concerns and fears develop after a myocardial infarction and affect the patient and his or her partner. Understanding by health professionals of the physiologic factors, the psychosocial adjustment, and the drug effects after myocardial infarction is vital for their patients.

PHYSIOLOGICAL ASPECTS

Most experts agree that there are few, if any, physiologic reasons for the cardiac patient not to achieve sexual satisfaction (Bakker, Bogdonoff and Hellerstein 1971). The physiologic effects of sexual intercourse have been systematically studied only in recent years. The data obtained from some studies (Masters and Johnson 1966) suggest that sexual activity is associated with marked cardiovascular fluctuations, including tachycardia ranging from 110 to 180/minute and impressive increases in blood pressure of 30 to 100 mm Hg systolic and 20 to 50 mm Hg diastolic. A study of post-myocardial infarction patients having sexual relations with their own mates in the privacy of their homes (Hellerstein and Friedman 1970) showed that the mean maximal heart rate during sexual activity corresponding to the phase of orgasm was 117.4/minute (range 90 to 144/minute). The mean heart rates for minute two and minute one, before the maximal heart rate, were 87/minute and 101.2/minute respectively, and for the minute one and minute two after the maximal heart rate, they were 96.9/minute and 85/minute. The blood pressures were calculated on the basis of pressures recorded during ergometric exercise on bicycles at the heart rates noted during sexual activity. The average systolic blood pressure while the patient was resting, prior to exercise on a bicycle, was 126.9 mm Hg and the average diastolic pressure was 85.1. The equivalent blood pressure during the maximal heart rate of sexual activity was 162/89 mm Hg. The patients were actually monitored by Holter (ECG) recording for 24 hours and the mean maximal heart rate during the performance of the usual occupational or professional activity was 120.1/minute (range 107 to 130/minute), which insignificantly exceeded that during sexual activity (117.4/minute). In six subjects the maximal heart rate during sexual activity exceeded that during work (127 vs. 117/minute), and in eight subjects it was less (110 vs. 122/minute). A later study (Nemec, Mansfield and Kennedy 1976) based on normal males 24 to 40 years of age, who volunteered to participate and had a Holter recording while having sexual relations with their wives in the privacy of their homes, revealed an average heart rate during orgasm of 114±14 beats/minute for the male superior position and 117±14 beats/minute for the female superior position. In a large study of patients exercised on a treadmill (Bruce et al. 1974) patients with angina and prior myocardial infarction reached a heart rate of 145±23/minute without developing symptoms. The levels reached by the patients in the study of Hellerstein and Friedman (1970) represent 81 percent of the heart rates reached on the treadmill. This means that the requirements for sexual activity are less than for activities that often produce symptoms.

In the study by Nemec and colleagues (1976) blood pressures were also recorded during sexual activity, by an automatic cuff inflating device. The blood pressures were 163±11 mm Hg systolic and 81±17 mm Hg diastolic, during the male-on-top position and 161±18 systolic and 77±12 diastolic during the male-on-bottom position. The results of this study failed to confirm the belief that the apparently more restful male-on-bottom position during sexual intercourse results in a lower increase in heart rate and blood pressure and is therefore preferable for cardiac patients.

It is generally safe to allow a patient to resume sexual activity if he or she can perform exercise at levels of 6 to 8 calories/minute without symptoms, abnormal pulse rate, or blood pressure or EKG changes (Hellerstein and Friedman 1970). These studies have shown that the equivalent oxygen cost of the maximal activity during sexual intercourse approximates 6 calories/minute (5 METs)* for less than 30 seconds and during the pre-orgasmic and post-orgasmic period, about 4.5 calories/minute. This is equivalent to what has been previously calculated, that the average energy cost for foreplay was 3.5 METs and for orgasm 5.5 METs (Douglas and Wilkes 1975). This energy is equal to what is needed for playing golf while carrying the clubs, playing doubles tennis, bicycling at 10 miles per hour, or raking leaves. The average patient who has recovered from an uncomplicated myocardial infarction has a maximum capacity of 8 to 9 METs. It has been stated by Hellerstein and Friedman (1970) that for lovemaking, the energy levels and demands placed on the heart are equal to walking briskly on the street or climbing one or two flights of stairs. A recent study (Larson et al. 1980) compared the heart rates and blood pressure responses to sexual activity and stair climbing in a group of nine healthy men and eight men with coronary artery disease with an average age of 50 years. The subjects walked for ten minutes on the level at a pace of 3 miles/hour and climbed 22 steps in 10 seconds. The study supported the clinical use of a two-flight stair climbing test (ten minutes of rapid walking followed by climbing two flights of stairs in ten seconds) as a physiologic test of readiness to resume sexual activity after an acute myocardial infarction. It should be stressed that the rate of climbing should be two steps per second and must be preceded by several minutes of rapid walking (120 paces/minute) to be an effective test. For the eight middle-aged coronary artery disease patients, the stair climbing test provided an adequate cardiovascular challenge with responses compatible to those of sexual activity. More accurate evaluation of the physical capacity of the patient can be estimated by the treadmill or bicycle exercise test, but one still has to consider that the response of coital heart rate cannot always be predicted with certainty because coitus requires isotonic and isometric effort and because the heart rate and blood pressure reflect additional factors, such as anxiety, fear, and excitement. The use of "mean" values for heart rate may also be inaccurate for a significant minority of patients. An ambulatory Holter (ECG) recorder, worn at home during coitus, will allow a direct evaluation of measured peak coital heart rate.

The effect of exercise training on the peak coital heart rate in post-myocardial infarction patients was studied by Stein (1977). Sixteen men (ages 46 to 54) underwent a 16-week bicycle ergometer training program 12 to 15 weeks following

---

Note: One MET is the basal oxygen requirement of the body in an inactive state, sitting quietly, considered to be 3.5 ml O_2/Kg/min.

their first myocardial infarction. Portable Holter (ECG) tape recorders were used to record the ECG during coitus before and after the training program. The maximum oxygen consumption was measured in each subject, during bicycle ergometer exercise, before and after the training program. The exercise trained group showed improvement with an increase in the maximum oxygen capacity of 11.5 percent and an average decrease in peak coital rate of 5.5 percent (from 127 to 120/minute). In a patient limited during coitus by anginal pain or other manifestations of ischemia, such a decrease in peak coital heart rate may be associated with a decrease in symptoms and a consequent improvement of sexual function.

Sexual activity with a partner and intercourse is not the only form of sexual expression of cardiac patients. Masturbation is not an uncommon sexual practice for individuals of many age groups, including those who have had myocardial infarction. A number of male patients may at times masturbate while still in the hospital. It is also felt that masturbation, as a therapeutic modality, may help the patient gain greater self-confidence in his own sexuality and facilitate the transition to sexual intercourse (Watts 1976). Masturbation, through the development of an erection, may provide to the male cardiac patient proof that his masculinity remains intact, as well as needed reassurance prior to the resumption of more stressful conjugal coital activity. Masturbatory activities of cardiac patients, however, were not studied for a long time. One report (Wagner 1975) stated that healthy young men when masturbating experienced a brief rise in heart rate to levels of 110 to 130/minute. In a controlled laboratory experiment (Sanderson, Held and Bohlen 1982) 11 healthy male and 11 healthy female subjects from 24 to 35 years old were monitored and their heart rates reported during repeated sessions of masturbation. The average resting heart rate was 68/minute. It increased an average of 29 percent during stimulation and 57 percent during orgasm. The mean peak heart rate during these sessions was 118/minute. Such factors as voluntary muscle tension and degree of fantasy may affect the increasing heart rates. These studies have not been replicated using subjects who actually have coronary artery disease.

A recent study (Bohlen et al. 1984) evaluated the heart rate, rate-pressure product (based on heart rate and systolic blood pressure), and oxygen uptake during four sexual activities of ten married couples that were studied at a research laboratory. Only the men's physiologic functions were monitored. They were studied during coitus with husband-on-top, coitus with wife-on-top, non-coital stimulation of husband by wife, and self-stimulation by husband. Maximum exercise values occurred during the brief response of orgasm (10 to 16 seconds), then returned quickly to near baseline levels. Cardiac and metabolic expenditures during stimulation and orgasm depended on the type of sexual activity. On average, the two non-coital activities had lower expenditures than the two coital positions; man-on-top coitus had the highest of the four activities. Their results agreed with those of Nemec, Mansfield and Kennedy (1976), that no significant difference exists during orgasm between man-on-top and man-on-bottom coitus for heart rate and rate-pressure product. However, the oxygen uptake differed between man-on-top and woman-on-top coitus. Still, the energy requirement, though averaged over the entire span of stimulation and orgasm, which was assumed to be less than the peak values, averaged a maximum of 4.4

METs. There was considerable variation in cardiac and metabolic expenditures, not only among the various sexual activities, but also among individuals' energy expenditures for the same activity.

The potential of cardiac arrhythmias during sexual activity exists, but it is small. In one study (Hellerstein and Friedman 1970) of 14 post-coronary patients who were monitored with Holter (ECG) recorders, ectopic premature beats occurred in three subjects (two ventricular, one ventricular and atrial) during sexual activity. In a study by Kavanagh and Shephard (1977) 3.7 percent of the post-myocardial infarction patients had premature ventricular beats and other types of arrhythmia during intercourse and 4.6 percent had them during the laboratory exercise test. In an evaluation of nine recent myocardial infarction patients by Holter (ECG) monitoring during sexual activity (Johnston and Fletcher 1979), one patient had premature ventricular beats but had similar arrhythmia throughout the 24-hour period of the recording, one patient had ventricular bigeminy and couplets of premature ventricular beats, and another premature atrial beats only during the period of coitus.

The cardiovascular response (ST-T changes or ectopic beats and symptoms) during coitus and occupational activities may be comparable in frequency and severity (Hellerstein and Friedman 1970). One of their several examples was a 52-year-old businessman with coronary artery disease and old infarction, who showed similar changes in heart rate and ECG during office work and during sexual activity. Marked displacement of the ST segment and occasional ventricular premature beats occurred during both activities.

The patient's sexual preferences and activities should be considered and discussed individually. The homosexual involvement of some patients cannot be ignored. Anal coitus has the potential of cardiac arrhythmias, not only to the active but also the passive partner. Bradycardia with syncope or sudden cardiac asystole have been observed during prostatic examination or massage, and electrocardiographic changes have been noted during sigmoidoscopic examinations and barium enemas (Beyer and Enos 1977).

PSYCHOLOGICAL ASPECTS

Unquestionably, an important factor that may affect the sexual function of patients after myocardial infarction is their psychological status. Soon after the onset of a heart attack psychological problems may develop. In a study of psychiatric evaluation of patients in a coronary care unit (Cassem and Hackett 1971) the three most frequent reasons for psychiatric referral were anxiety, depression, and behavior management. The focus of anxiety was impending death or death's heralds: pain, breathlessness, weakness, and new complications. Depression followed injury to self-esteem caused by the heart attack. Most management problems stemmed from excessive denial of illness, inappropriate euphoric or sexual behavior, and hostile-dependent conflicts with the staff.

Depression is one of the main psychiatric complications of convalescence (Hackett and Cassem 1975), which may be due to several restraints binding the convalescent cardiac patient: the threat of recurrence and possible sudden death;

inactivity and job uncertainty; deprivation or limitation of food, alcohol, excitement, and sex; and depression due to possible disruption of interpersonal relationships. The patient may develop anxiety and fears after discharge from the hospital. Fears have been described by patients in various studies and the incidence varied from 18 to 51 percent (Tuttle, Cook and Fitch 1964; Amsterdam et al. 1977; Papadopoulos et al. 1983). Hackett and Cassem (1975) emphasized that some of the fears were due to common myths: even mild exercise is dangerous; sexual intercourse should never be attempted because following a myocardial infarction one is "over the hill"; repeated infarction or sudden death is more likely to occur at sexual orgasm; driving must be avoided; the arms must not be suddenly raised above the head; the patient is apt to die at the same age as the parent who had a heart attack; recurrence is apt to take place around the anniversary of the first infarction; the heart is more vulnerable to repeat infarctions and sudden death while the patient sleeps.

Fear of resumption of sexual activity was expressed by 31 percent of our male patients and 51 percent of our female patients (Papadopoulos 1978; Papadopoulos et al. 1983). Such fears were not uncommon among spouses, varying from 44 to 68 percent (Papadopoulos 1978; Papadopoulos et al. 1980; Papadopoulos et al. 1983). The major fears expressed about resuming sexual activity were chest pain, another heart attack, coital death, poor quality of sexual activity, sexual unattractiveness of the patient to the partner after the heart attack, or discovery of a previously existing illicit sexual relationship of the patient.

Fear of sexual activity was frequently mentioned as a cause of no resumption of sexual activity, but this was often not statistically significant between the group that resumed sexual activity and the group that did not. Other factors, such as the age of the couple, the number of years of marriage, the previous sexual drive, and the level of interpersonal communication between the couple had a strong effect on resumption. Fear, however, was a reason that would decrease the frequency of sexual activity or affect the quality. Fears of resumption were expressed by female patients more often than by males (Papadopoulos et al. 1983), which may accurately assess the situation or simply reflect denial among male patients.

In a review of the psychological aspects of ischemic heart disease (Mayou 1978) it was stated that even though many patients had returned to the work they did before, they usually reduced their leisure activities to a major extent and made changes in marriage, family life, social family, and sexual activity.

In a study of the emotional reaction, health preoccupation, and sexual activity two months after a myocardial infarction (Wiklund et al. 1984) 65 percent of patients felt anxious and depressed. Fatigue and nervousness were regarded by the patients as more disabling than cardiac symptoms. Emotional distress was related to a previous history of emotional complaints and to psychological factors and self-reported coronary symptoms, but it was unrelated to the severity of the infarction, medically rated cardiac symptoms, and demographic and social data. Sexual maladjustment, mainly due to fear, was frequent and associated with both emotional and somatic variables.

In another report of 68 patients (Stern, Pascale and Ackerman 1977) the frequency of sexual activity decreased in approximately 20 percent of patients, the majority of whom were either anxious or depressed as well. Fourteen patients in the group were females. They took a longer time to return to work (13.5 weeks vs. 7.9 weeks) and sexual functioning (11.5 weeks vs. 6.1 weeks) than male patients. At one year, only 40 percent were actively engaged in sexual functioning compared with 93 percent for the men. Anxiety and/or depression was present in 80 percent of the women. A possible explanation took into account the specific psychosocial pattern of these women, demonstrating a higher degree of type A behavior than the corresponding group of post-infarction men.

The significance of psychological factors in the resumption of sexual activity is also emphasized by the absence of correlation between work capacity and sexual relations (Bloch, Maeder and Haissly 1975). Some patients with great physical fitness had no more sexual activity, while others continued to have frequent intercourse in spite of poor physical capacity.

PHARMACOLOGICAL ASPECTS

Cardiovascular drugs that the coronary patients may be taking can affect their sexuality (Papadopoulos 1980). Diuretics, antihypertensives, anti-arrhythmics, anti-anginals, and hypolipidemics may have sexual side effects in some patients. They may result in diminished libido, impotence, ejaculatory and orgasmic difficulties, inhibited vaginal lubrication, menstrual irregularities, and gynecomastia in men or painful breast enlargement in women. Other medications that the coronary patients may be taking, such as sedatives, antidepressants, tranquilizers, antispasmodics, and histamine H_2 receptor antagonists may also have negative sexual impact in certain patients.

On the other hand, these medications may often have a beneficial effect on the sexuality of some patients. In cases of patients with angina during sexual activity, the use of beta blockers and sublingual nitrates have proven beneficial. Anti-arrhythmic drugs in patients who develop arrhythmias during sexual activity may reduce the concern of the patients who have palpitations during intercourse. Antihypertensive medications, when properly selected, by controlling the blood pressure in hypertensive patients, may allow better quality of sexual life. Psychotropic drugs may alleviate the anxiety or depression of the patient and allow him or her a more normal approach to sexual life.

THE SPOUSE OF THE POST-CORONARY PATIENT

Marriage has a legal and religious status, but at the same time has physiological, psychological and sociological components. Sexual activity is part of the long-term mutual commitment of marriage, and the impact of a myocardial infarction on this and other aspects of marital relationship is often significant.

The patient's spouse is often subjected to a tremendous amount of stress. Role reversal occurs in both the family and the marital unit, which often persists after hospitalization and during the home bound phase of recovery and is a threat to the patient's sexuality (Okoniewski 1979). A wife may be unable to cope with the demands of her husband, which are frequently indications of depression or denial of his illness. She feels both guilty and hostile regarding her possible contribution to her husband's condition. If the wife is the patient, the husband is also subjected to increased stress. He is often forced to assume the role of both mother and father in the home and he may be unable to simultaneously meet the demands of being both breadwinner and running a household. He may also feel guilty or hostile. These feelings often make communication about sexual and non-sexual matters difficult. Interpersonal conflicts develop in both stable and unstable pre-illness marital units (Wishnie, Hackett and Cassem 1971).

In a review of the psychological consequences of myocardial infarction on 65 wives of male patients, 38 percent found the period of convalescence after discharge very stressful and attributed this to fears of a recurrent infarction and marital tension because of their husbands' increased irritability and dependency (Skelton and Dominian 1973). These anxieties and tensions gradually diminished, and at one year after the initial illness, only eight wives whose husbands had made a good physical recovery still showed considerable psychological disturbance. The impact of the illness appeared to depend on the quality of the marital relations before its onset. When there was evidence of problems before the illness, in most cases the difficulties were exacerbated by the infarction. Four wives, however, who had previous problems felt that improvement in their husbands' moods after the illness resulted in a noticeable improvement in their relations. Many wives felt that the frequency of sexual intercourse had been decreasing as they became older and the illness only accelerated this trend. Nine wives, however, expressed concern and anxiety about the effect of intercourse on their husbands and wanted to discuss the problem and seek advice. These were the spouses who enjoyed sexual intercourse and wanted to resume relations, as before the illness. They thought that it was their anxiety about the safety of sexual intercourse on their husbands' health that was responsible for the decline in sexual activity.

A study of 82 wives of men suffering a first myocardial infarction revealed that they had substantial and persistent psychological symptoms and the husband's illness had continuing effects on their work, leisure and social activities, and family life and marriage; their psychosocial disability was compatible to that of the patients (Mayou, Foster and Williamson 1978). For many wives it had been a difficult year; their husbands had been depressed, frustrated, and irritable, and the stresses had brought some marriages to a breaking point. Although nearly half the couples reported an unchanged level of sexual activity, there was much anxiety and lack of confidence; a quarter had less frequent intercourse and a quarter had virtually none.

Our report based on interviews with 100 wives of post-myocardial infarction patients revealed that the wives' sexual concerns were the risk of intercourse; the sexual difficulties of the husbands and change in sexual patterns; the patients' symptoms during intercourse; the emotional relationship of the couple; and poor sexual instructions by the health professionals (Papadopoulos et al. 1983). While their husbands were still hospitalized, 31 wives stated that they had concerns about future sexual activity. Most of them wondered whether intercourse would be too strenuous. After discharge of the patients, all of the wives developed concerns and nearly all who were fearful of resuming sexual activity expressed fear of the husband having chest pain or another heart attack. Some feared coital death. A 46-year-old wife, married to a 63-year-old man for 26 years, stated that she was afraid her husband "would get tired and have another heart attack since he gets shortness of breath easily." They never resumed sexual activity.

Several wives, in a group of 24 who did not resume sexual activity, expressed sexual anxieties and frustrations. A couple in their late fifties, married for 39 years, were sexually active before the heart attack, having had intercourse once a week. The wife stated that since his attack they had tried to have intercourse but were unsuccessful because of the husband's impotence. She stated that she is frustrated and "really misses sex since she always enjoyed it." Such emotional burdens may cause the wife to react with despondency or anger to her mate's illness and the change in their sexual relationship. This may have a disorganizing effect on him and his performance.

Other wives, however, saw the termination of sexual relations as an opportunity to end previously unwelcome sexual activity. Of a couple, both 56 years old, who were married 33 years the wife stated that they had not resumed sexual activity since his heart attack, three years earlier. She does not have any real sexual desire. Her husband has not made any sexual attempt and she has not encouraged him to do so. She is "just as glad not to bother with sex."

According to the reports of the wives, the patient-husbands developed symptoms during intercourse in 29 percent of the cases (Papadopoulos et al. 1980). This percentage is lower than percentages from data reported by male patients in other studies (Hellerstein and Friedman 1970; Papadopoulos 1978). It probably reflects the fact that the wife is not always aware of the patient's symptoms and he often does not report them to her. The wives stated that their reactions to coital symptoms of their husbands were fear, anxiety and, in a few cases, guilt. A 36-year-old wife married to a 39-year-old man stated that at times during intercourse he would develop pain in his chest and down the left arm. This would make her fearful and anxious and they would stop their sexual activity.

We found a statistically significant association between the emotional relationship of the husband and wife and the resumption of sexual activity. Failure to sexually communicate often leads to communication failure in other areas of marriage. In the group that did not resume sexual activity, 8 percent had a closer emotional relationship after the myocardial infarction, while 54 percent had a more distant relationship. In the group that resumed sexual activity, 47 percent had a closer emotional relationship after the cardiac event and 17 percent a more distant one (Papadopoulos et al. 1980). In some cases the closer emotional relationship that developed after the myocardial infarction led to a better sexual relationship. In other cases, the sequence was the reverse. A 39-year-old wife whose husband is 42 years old, married for 20 years, stated that they increased the frequency of intercourse from twice a week to three times a week after he had his heart attack. The wife felt that their sexual relationship made him feel more sure of himself and this brought a closer emotional rapport. They talk more now. He has taken time to look at his life and readjust his schedule, spending more time with his family, and he is "more fun and more loving."

Many wives felt that they had not received adequate instructions and information about sexual activity. Some were told "take it easy" or "it is all right to resume sexual activity as long as it is not strenuous." Less than half of the wives received any sexual information before the spouse's discharge and only a few got sexual instructions from a physician. In some cases the information was provided by a nurse or by printed material. The women believed that the information they received about sexual activity was incomplete. Apparently, even when the health professional approaches the subject of sexual activity after a myocardial infarction, he or she is reluctant to discuss it in detail. This may be due to the person's attitude toward sex, inadequate preparation for dealing with topics of sexuality, or lack of familiarity with the available data.

About half of the couples reported a change in technique or position, referring mainly to avoidance of previously used positions. Elimination of variation of sexual activity was accepted by the wives, although by many with frustration. Very few couples started using new positions and the rest made no changes.

CORONARY COITAL DEATH

At times one of the fears expressed by coronary patients and their spouses is the threat of death during intercourse. Anecdotal cases of celebrities dying under such circumstances reported by the media or instances of coital death incorporated in romantic television shows have perpetuated the fear of coital death as a common event. One patient clearly stated that she was afraid she "would die while having intercourse" because she often watched in soap operas "people dying while having sex after a heart attack."

This topic has been much debated and unfortunately it has not been addressed in a systematic way. "Coital death" or "death in the saddle" or as the French have romantically called it, "La Mort d'Amour (love death)" has often been argued as a fact or fiction. There is no question that such cases occur and many physicians are aware of individual instances.

Accurate data are often difficult to obtain since the partner in illicit relationships disappears and then calls the police, and in marital situations the wife may be hesitant to report the real circumstances. The private physician often signs the death certificate without inquiring into the exact circumstances under which the death occurred.

In 1973 when we contacted the postmortem medical examiners' offices of the various states, we realized the paucity of organized information in regard to sudden cardiac deaths and specifically the circumstances under which they occurred. We were able to collect 20 anecdotal cases, however, which were attributed to heart disease and in 15 (75 percent) of those cases the event occurred during extramarital intercourse. Experiences of the medical examiners are that when such cases come to their attention, they usually occur in an illicit sexual connection, in unfamiliar surroundings, and after a large meal and high alcohol intake. Superimposed on the demands of the sexual act during the digestive process, is the psychologic effect of sexual excitement, guilt, fear, or discovery and the concern over possible impotence (Massie et al. 1969).

Although the true incidence of new infarction or sudden death during intercourse is difficult to establish, a study conducted in Japan (Ueno 1963) indicated that coitus accounted for only 34 of 5,559 cases (0.6 percent) of sudden death. Death was due to heart disease in about half of these 34 cases (0.3 percent), and in 24 (70 percent) it occurred during or after intercourse with a partner other than the wife and in a place other than the home. Excessive alcohol intake was noted in 12 of the 34 cases.

An American pathologist working in a medical examiner's office estimated and was quoted in the report of Hellerstein and Friedman (1970), that in his experience sexual activity was associated with sudden death in approximately three of 500 subjects with arteriosclerotic heart disease (0.6 percent).

In a study of 100 sudden deaths from coronary artery disease (Myers and Dewar 1975) "no patient was recorded as having died soon after or during coitus." The most significant relationship of sudden death was with acute psychological stress. A recent meal, especially if accompanied by high alcohol consumption, was also significantly related.

Excitement has often been considered an additional factor in the increased rate of sudden death during extramarital relations, after a myocardial infarction. In a report of Holter (ECG) recording during sexual activity, Johnston and Fletcher (1979) included a post-coronary bypass patient who experienced sexual activity twice during a 24-hour period. During coitus with his girlfriend, at noon, a heart rate of 96 to 150/minute with occasional premature ventricular beats was noted. During coitus with his wife, in the evening, normal sinus rhythm with rates of 72 to 92/minute and no premature beats were recorded.

On the other hand, a man having sexual intercourse with his mistress of many years may have no difficulty, but he may have enhanced cardiovascular response when resuming sexual activity with a spouse after a long period of abstinence.

The association of emotional stress and sudden death has been described in several cases (Malik 1973). Twenty-two reliably documented cases of sudden coronary deaths were described, related to a range of emotional behavior patterns, including anger, grief, depression, fright, and excitement. Beyond emotional stress, the patient's age, status of the myocardium, the potential for arrhythmias, the physiological effort involved in the sexual activity, and any other factors that may increase this load and the status of the central nervous system — particularly the activity of the sympathetic nervous system — may play a role in inducing coital death.

A series of studies that document stimulation of high sympathetic nerve centers as being involved in the production of arrhythmias and ventricular fibrillation have been published (De Silva and Lown 1978).

The concept of "sexual analgesia" leading to coital death has been considered (Nalbantgil et al. 1976). Coronary patients had marked ST depression in Holter (ECG) recordings during sexual activity and no chest pain or discomfort, while they suffered from precordial pain during other exercise, with fewer ST depressions and a lesser degree of tachycardia.

The status of "coital death" was summarized a few years ago (Derogatis and King 1981). It was stated that we know there has been no systematic research on the issue of coital death in the cardiac patient and that the best available study is now many years old (Ueno 1963); we believe the physiological demands of sexuality are minimal to modest for the cardiac patient who has passed the acute stage of illness and that cardiac arrhythmia is the cause of death in the large majority of cases. The authors added that one can suspect that sexual activity may possess unique risks for fatal arrhythmia and hypothesize that these risks are associated with the intense sympathetic nervous activity inherent in sexual behavior and the concomitant increase in blood catecholamines. An evaluation of conjugal sexual coronary deaths is still needed.

SEX AND ANGINA

Patients who have coronary artery disease may experience angina pectoris during sexual activity. Most of them may also have chest discomfort or pain during other daily activities, while occasional patients may exhibit the symptoms only during or after sexual intercourse. Physiological, psychological, and environmental factors may play a role in precipitating the symptoms. Sexual activity after strenuous exercise, after a heavy meal or excessive intake of alcohol, much excitement and fear, or intercourse in a cold or hot and humid room may cause an undue increase in blood pressure and heart rate, which causes angina. On the other hand, when such factors are minimal during sexual activity, the patient may have an asymptomatic sexual relation, though he or she experiences symptoms during other activities. The possibility of an "analgesic effect of sexual activity" has also been promulgated in such patients, when the ECG changes of ischemia occur during sex, without concomitant chest pain (Nalbantgil et al. 1976).

Patients who may have angina during intercourse may decide to abstain from sexual activity, either because of the discomfort or because of the fear that this may lead to a heart attack or sudden death.

Jackson (1980) reported on his experiences in managing 35 patients with stable angina pectoris, who were questioned about their sexual activity. Twenty-nine patients (83 percent) had intercourse more than once a week and 6 (17 percent) abstained. Of those who were sexually active, 19 (65 percent) developed chest pain on most occasions. All of them and their spouses worried about the pain and felt that it interfered with the frequency and enjoyment of sexual intercourse. Four of the 19 also complained about palpitations during intercourse. All the patients received sexual instructions and basic advice in regard to preparing themselves and their environment for intercourse. They were advised to warm the bedroom and the sheets and to avoid intercourse soon after a meal or a bath. They were all started on beta-blocking drugs and if they still had pain during sexual activity, they were to take 5 or 10 mg. isosorbide dinitrate, sublingually, 10 minutes prior to intercourse. Of the 35 patients, only two were not enjoying pain-free sexual intercourse after the specific management.

Patients with angina pectoris during sexual activity should have a cardiac medical evaluation, including determination of coronary risk factors, an exercise treadmill or bicycle ergometer test, and a Holter (ECG) monitor recording. There will be some patients, who based on their symptoms and the significance of the results of the exercise test, may also require coronary angiography.

Beta-blocker medications taken orally or a transdermal nitroglycerin patch applied in the evening or sublingual use of nitroglycerin just prior to sexual activity, and warming the bed sheets may provide symptom-free sexual relations. Use of anti-arrhythmics for cases of significant arrhythmia, detected by Holter recording, is recommended. Participation in an exercise program prescribed specifically on the basis of the exercise test results will alleviate chest discomfort and improve sexual physical tolerance.

REHABILITATION AND SEXUAL COUNSELING

Rehabilitation implies achievement by the patient of his or her optimal levels of physical, mental, vocational, and social activities; resumption of sexual physical activity is an important aspect. After a myocardial infarction, the patient's self-image is affected, not only as a parent and breadwinner, but also as a sexual partner. Attention to the sexual concerns and needs of the post-coronary patient and the partner is vital for complete rehabilitation. In most cases of myocardial infarction sexual activity may be gradually integrated into the program of physical and psychological rehabilitation.

Rehabilitation of the patient should start as soon as he or she is medically stable. A progressive increase in physical activity before and after discharge from the hospital, based on stress exercise tests and complimented by the appropriate participation in exercise programs, will provide the patient with improved physical tolerance, which will give him or her self-confidence and an improved sense of well-being. Studies have shown that during training programs the patients improved physically (Hellerstein and Friedman 1970; Kavanagh and Shephard 1977; Stein 1977). Other studies have shown less mental depression in post-myocardial infarction patients after reconditioning (Hackett and Cassem 1973).

It is vital for the physician, the nurse, and the other health professionals to appreciate the negative impact of myocardial infarction on the sexuality of patients and to provide the needed counseling. Too often the psychosexual effects of myocardial infarction on the patient are neglected because of the overriding concern for the medical aspects of the illness or a lack of time. Usually the emphasis of counseling is on diet and weight reduction, cessation of smoking, and physical activity plans. Discussion of sexual activity is often neglected. Patient and family education curricula should include the following (Wenger 1981):

1. A brief review of normal cardiac structure and function and of the atherosclerotic process causing coronary obstruction.
2. Dispelling prevalent myths regarding the precipitation of myocardial infarction.
3. Insight into behavior patterns that may affect the risk of reinfarction and into the value of altering these habits.
4. The rationale for dietary changes — calorie, fat, sodium restriction.
5. Cessation of cigarette smoking.
6. Physical activity plans.
7. Resumption of sexual activity, using the guideline that sexual intercourse is appropriate and safe when other usual daily activities are reinstituted. Both partners should be counseled about the resumption of sexual activity.
8. Control of associated disease, particularly hypertension and diabetes mellitus and of other coronary risk factors.
9. Medications to be taken at home.

10. The appropriate response to new or recurrent symptoms.
11. Teaching cardiopulmonary resuscitation to families of myocardial infarction survivors.
12. Community resources that may be helpful. These include counseling services, home-care agencies, etc.
13. Family counseling, including lifestyle adjustments during convalescence.

The number of patients fearful and requesting sexual counseling remains high (Papadopoulos 1978; Papadopoulos et al. 1983; Miller, Gossard and Taylor 1984). If sexuality occupied an important place in the lives of these patients and their partners, then specific information on the return to sexual functioning should be included in the rehabilitation process (McLane, Krop and Mehta 1980). It is important that physicians provide a sensitive atmosphere so that patients with sexual concerns will be sufficiently comfortable to express them. The physician must also recognize that some patients will not be able to introduce the topic of sex, regardless of the quality of patient-physician communication and should be prepared to approach the subject as a matter of routine. Physicians and other health professionals should be aware that not all patients will have problems after a myocardial infarction and some who report no sexual problems may be denying their existence.

A sexual history obtained, as part of the data base, from all cardiac patients is important in providing counseling, as is thorough sexual instruction of the post-coronary patient and his or her partner with specific attention to their sexual concerns and needs.

Sexual instructions to the patient should be based on their previous sexual history. Sexual preferences, desires, and concerns should also be explored. In considering the patient's sexual response to the disease, the premorbid state of the individual, the physiopathologic effect of the disease process, the psychologic state of the patient, the effect of treatment upon the patient, and the response of the marital partner to the illness should be considered (Dengrove 1968). Furthermore, we believe that the age of the patient, the duration of marriage, the previous sexual drive, and previous sexual satisfaction are significant factors in the interest and the decision of the patient to resume sexual activity. The presence of such associated conditions as hypertension and diabetes mellitus may also affect the patient.

Most patients and their spouses believe that sexual instructions and counseling should be provided by the physician and a nurse before discharge from the hospital (Horgan and Craig 1978; Papadopoulos et al. 1980; Papadopoulos et al. 1983).

Sexual instructions are often not specific and comprehensive and may not alleviate the fears of the patient (Papadopoulos 1978; Papadopoulos et al. 1980; Papadopoulos et al. 1983). The physician should, in discussing the subject of sex, avoid generalities and answer questions concerning the resumption of coitus, coital position, frequency, and the side effects of drug therapy. Non-specific advice, such as "you may resume sex, but take it easy" or "don't worry," may only create more anxiety and fear. The physician should be responsive to the patient's sexual needs and add "educator" and "counselor" to the more traditional roles of "diagnostician" and "therapist" (Stein 1984). The physician should tailor his or her remarks and style of presentation to the individual patient and family, taking into account their anxiety level, intelligence, and mood.

Often recall of information and advice by the patient is low (Mayou, Williamson and Foster 1976). Several reasons, such as lack of an appropriate hospital area for communication and discussion with the patient and the spouse, the physical and mental state of the patient, inadequate method of communication, and uncertainty of the counselor about appropriate advice may contribute to this deficiency.

Very often, advice about sexual activity after myocardial infarction is provided through printed material, without consideration of the patient's ability to read and comprehend. In one review, the patients' mean reading and comprehension abilities were at the eighth-grade level, which indicated that they probably could not read and understand the current lay cardiovascular literature available to them (Boyd and Feldman 1984). The patients' preferred learning style was one to one interaction with doctors and nurses. We believe that specific instructions given to the patient in written form and explained clearly may provide the best method of comprehensible and effective communication.

Sexual counseling should be supportive and reassuring to the couple and should strive to facilitate communication between the patient and the partner. Failure to sexually communicate often leads to communication failure in other areas of the marriage. The quality of family life and marriage are markedly associated with sexual satisfaction and appear to be important determinants of the psychological and social outcome for the patient (Mayou, Foster and Williamson 1978). Most of the wives of male patients (Papadopoulos et al. 1980) prefer to receive sexual instructions together with their husbands and have the opportunity to explore their concerns and fears. This may reduce some of the interpersonal conflicts that may emerge in previously stable, as well as unstable, marital units (Wishnie, Hackett and Cassem 1971). One year after the myocardial infarction the wives continued to influence the rate and extent of convalescence of their spouses (Mayou, Foster and Williamson 1978). The wife plays a major role in the patient's coping, adaptation, and readjustment and in his future physical and emotional health; therefore, attention to her sexual concerns and needs is vital. Ignoring the spouse can only be counterproductive to successful cardiovascular rehabilitation.

Nurses may play a vital role in counseling of the spouses during hospitalization of their partners and thereafter, visiting them and the patient in their homes after discharge, since public health nurses are in a strong position to assist family relationships during the recuperation period and to offer help when it is needed (Larter 1976). Currently, home health agencies may provide such services through trained nurses.

Wives or husbands who were looking for an acceptable rationalization for ending sexual activity that was unsatisfactory can use health concerns to serve this purpose. When a wife or husband indicates concern about continuing sexual relations, the interviewer must take a careful sexual history to help determine if the concern is genuine or merely an excuse for stopping the unwanted activity. If previous sexual relations were truly satisfactory and mutually enjoyable, it is likely that the concern is genuine.

The physician should meet with the patient and the partner before discharge from the hospital and openly and in an authoritative way discuss the issue of sexual activity. He or she should offer open-ended questions, such as, "How do you feel about resuming your usual activities, like going back to work, enjoying hobbies, and having sex?" The physician should be ready to provide assurance about the ability to resume sexual activity and reassure them that whenever there is any question as to the ability of the patient this can be further evaluated by special exercise tests and by Holter (ECG) monitoring during sexual activity.

There are certain assessment topics that may be used to provide the baseline information needed to individualize the instructions for the patient and the sexual partner (Scalzi 1982):

1. Assessment of the patient's past experience with chest pain during sexual stimulation and/or intercourse. If the patient has experienced symptoms during sexual activity prior to his or her myocardial infarction, one can anticipate increased fear and anxiety associated with the resumption of this activity.

    Ability to participate without symptoms in an exercise test up to 6 METs may reassure the couple. Participation in a progressive exercise program and use of medications may also increase the confidence and physical tolerance of the patient.

2. Assessment of a previous history of sexual difficulty prior to the heart attack, such as impotence or premature ejaculation, and the circumstances under which it occurred should be evaluated. Periodic episodes of sexual difficulty are normal and commonly associated with fatigue and emotional stress. Nevertheless sexual difficulty prior to myocardial infarction tends to increase the patient's fear of further sexual difficulty and permanent impotence. Assessment of the medications the patient was taking prior to the infarction is important since they could have caused the difficulty.

3. Assessment of the patient and partner's understanding of when they can resume sexual activity. It is important to identify their expectations, the information they have already acquired, and their misconceptions, all of which may need to be clarified when providing instructions.

We believe that beyond the initial sexual counseling before discharge from the hospital, there should be further followup at the first visit of the patient to the physician's office and periodically thereafter, as necessary. Nurses, through rehabilitation programs and home visits, may also be of great assistance. When reservations, ambiguities, or anxieties persist beyond four to six weeks after the start of counseling and continue to block progress, complex interpersonal psychopathology should be considered and may require more analytical or specialized behavior techniques. At this point, referral to a psychiatrist or psychologist experienced in the management of sexual dysfunction may be indicated (Cooper 1985).

For a couple that wishes to restart sexual activity the following general advice could be given:

Time of resumption.

When a patient's condition has been stable and he or she is asymptomatic, sexual activity may be resumed within three to six weeks. The time, however, may vary depending on the libido of the involved couple. It should be pointed out that the extent of recovery from sexual inertia or from other causes of unsuccessful coitus depends upon the duration of the period of abstinence (Cooper 1985). An exercise program may encourage an earlier return to sexual activity. Women, however, are less likely to participate in structured cardiac rehabilitation programs and also seem to resume sexual activity later than men (Boogaard 1984). Menopause is another factor that may influence the return of a female patient to sexual activity because of certain psychological and physiological changes that may occur. Studies done in recent years have shown a wide spectrum of reactions to menopause, ranging from a non-specific sense of liberation to a feeling of loss of femininity and sexual desire (Dyer 1979).

Initial contacts.

In the first contact with the partner non-demand, non-genital, touching should be encouraged and in some cases masturbation to partial arousal should be allowed. This may build the patient's self-confidence, provided there are no complaints of chest pain, shortness of breath, or palpitations. Non-orgasmic, exciting forms of stimulation should be progressively repeated and extended over the next week. As the libido and confidence of the patient increase and he or she remains physically comfortable, it is permissible to proceed with coitus. Foreplay is desirable and as important as the "warm-up" period before any exercise. Rest preceding sexual activity and intercourse is advisable and often marital relations may be preferable after a good sleep.

Partner.

The patient may be reassured that the return to sexual activity with a long-term partner will not involve any excessive physical or emotional demand on the heart.

Environment.

Sexual activity in the usual surroundings of one's home and comfortable room is advisable. Extremes of air temperatures, humidity, restrictive clothing, and cold bed sheets should be avoided.

Other precautions.

Avoid active sexual activity and intercourse soon after physical or emotional stress, after eating a heavy meal, and after drinking excessive alcohol.

Positions.

It is not invariably necessary to recommend transition to unfamiliar sexual positions, especially if the patient may feel that this affects his masculine or her feminine role. Most patients do not make changes in patterns of foreplay or position adopted during coitus (Kavanagh and Shephard 1977; Papadopoulos et al. 1980). However, if it is acceptable to the couple, the patient may assume the bottom position, which may be more restful or the patient may consider the side-by-side, face to back position. In certain situations, especially if the patient develops shortness of breath when lying down, he or she may be more relaxed sitting in a chair with the partner sitting on the patient's lap.

Warning signals.

The patient should know and report to his or her physician rapid heart rate and rapid heart breathing that persist for ten to fifteen minutes after coitus; a feeling of extreme fatigue that may persist until the next day; irregular heart beating, dizziness, lightheadedness or "blacking out"; chest pain during or after coitus; and sexual dysfunction.

The patient must discontinue smoking, try to control his or her weight, and progressively increase physical activity or participate in a supervised exercise program. If a question arises concerning the patient's physical tolerance and possibility of an arrhythmia, a treadmill or bicycle ergometer stress exercise test or a Holter (ECG) monitor recording during the time of sexual activity can provide objective evaluation for appropriate guidance and medical treatment, as needed, and the use of anti-anginal and anti-arrhythmic medications, when necessary.

The patient will deal better with sexual relations if the anxiety or depression that he or she may experience are recognized by the physician and encouragement and reassurance are provided. Enrollment in a cardiac rehabilitation program or in a support group for post-infarction patients may be beneficial. When necessary, anxiolytic or antidepressant drugs should be used (Stern 1985).

When the patient's condition is stable and the couple eager to resume sexual activity, but there is persistent sexual dysfunction, referral for sexual therapy is indicated. Increasing attention and clinical application of sexual therapy to patients with physical illness have a favorable effect (Scalzi, Loya and Golden 1977).

Certain couples, who because of fear or sexual dysfunction would not be interested in intercourse, should be reassured that the expression of affection by cuddling and caressing may be rewarding.

At a time when the life of the patient and the partner is heavily burdened with fears and anxieties, proper counseling by well-informed physicians, nurses, and other health professionals will lead to successful rehabilitation and alleviate much of the stress that can interfere with their emotional and sexual life.

BIBLIOGRAPHY

American Heart Association. 1988. "Heart Facts." Dallas: AHA Office of Communications.

Amsterdam, E. A., Amsterdam, G., Riggs, L. K. et al. 1977. "Sexual counseling and sexual activity after myocardial infarction: Patients' attitudes and physician response." (Abstract) *Clin Res* 25:86A.

Bakker, C., Bogdonoff, M., Hellerstein, H. 1971. "Heart disease and sex response to questions." *Med Asp of Hum Sex* 5:24–35.

Beyer, J. C., Enos, W. F. 1977. "Obscure causes of death during sexual activity." *Med Asp of Hum Sex* 14:81–94.

Bloch, A., Maeder, J. P., Haissly, J. C. 1975. "Sexual problems after myocardial infarction." *Am Heart J* 90:536–37.

Bohlen, J. G., Held, J. P., Sanderson, M. O. et al. 1984. "Heart rate, rate-pressure product, and oxygen uptake during four sexual activities." *Arch Intern Med* 144: 1745–48.

Boogaard, M. A. K. 1984. "Rehabilitation of the female patient after myocardial infarction." *Nurs Clin North Am* 19:433–40.

Boyd, M. D., Feldman, R. H. L. 1984 "Health information seeking and reading and comprehension abilities of cardiac rehabilitation patients." *J Cardiac Rehab* 4:343–47.

Bruce, R. A., Fisher, L. D., Cooper, M. N. et al. 1974. "Separation of effects of cardiovascular disease and age on ventricular function with maximal exercise." *Am J. Cardiol* 34:757–63.

Cassem, N. H., Hackett, T. P. 1971. "Psychiatric consultation in a coronary care unit." *Ann of Int Med* 75:9–14.

Cooper, A. J. 1985. "Myocardial infarction and advice on sexual activity." *The Practitioner* 229:575–79.

Datey, K. K. 1977. "Sex and heart disease." *J Assoc Phys Ind* 25:647–52.

Dengrove, E. 1968. "Sexual responses to disease processes." *J Sex Res* 4:257–66.

Derogatis, L. R., King, K. M., 1981. "The coital coronary: A reassessment of the concept." *Arch of Sex Beh* 10:325–35.

DeSilva, R. A., Lown, B. 1978. "Ventricular premature beats, stress and sudden death." *Psychosomatics* 19:649–61.

Douglas, J. E., Wilkes, T. D. 1975. "Reconditioning cardiac patients." *Amer Fam Phys* 11:123–29.

Dyer, R. 1979. "Menopause — a closer look for nurses." In *Women in stress: A nursing perspective,* edited by D. Kjervik and I. Martinson, pp. 303–18. New York: Appleton-Century-Crofts.

Grand, A., Delorme, P., Tabet-Derraz, R. 1982. "Sexual behavior of coronary patients after myocardial infarction." *Arch Mal Coeur* 75:1215–21.

Gupta, M. C., Singh, M. M. 1982. "Postinfarction sexual activity." *J Ind Med Assoc* 79:45–48.

Hackett, T. P., Cassem, N. H. 1973. "Psychological adaptation to convalescence in myocardial infarction patients." In *Exercise testing and exercise training in coronary heart disease,* edited by J. Naughton, H. Hellerstein and I. Mohler, pp. 253–62. New York: Academic Press.

____. 1975. "Psychological management of the myocardial infarction patient." *J of Hum Stress* 11:25–38.

Hellerstein, H. K., Friedman, E. H. 1970. "Sexual activity and the postcoronary patient." *Arch Int Med* 125:987–99.

Horgan, J. H., Craig, A. J. 1978. "Resumption of sexual activity after myocardial infarction." *J of Irish Med Assoc* 71:540–42.

Jackson, G. 1980. "Sexual intercourse and angina pectoris." *Int Rehab Med* 3:35–37.

Johnston, B. L., Fletcher, G. F. 1979. "Dynamic electrocardiographic recording during sexual activity in recent post-myocardial infarction and revascularization patients." *Am Heart J* 98:736–41.

Kavanagh, T., Shephard, R. J. 1977. "Sexual activity after myocardial infarction." *Can Med Assoc J* 116:1250–53.

Larson, J. L., McNaughton, M. W., Kennedy, J. W., et al. 1980. "Heart rate and blood pressure responses to sexual activity and a stair-climbing test." *Heart & Lung* 9:1025–30.

Larter, M. H. 1976. "M.I. wives need you." *RN* 39:44–48.

Malik, M. A. O. 1973. "Emotional stress as a precipitating factor in sudden deaths due to coronary insufficiency." *J Forensic Sci* 18(1):47–52.

Mann, S., Yates, J. E., Raftery, E. B. 1981. "The effects of myocardial infarction on sexual activity." *J Cardiac Rehab* 1:187–93.

Massie, E., Rose, E. F., Rupp, J. C. et al. 1969. "Sudden death during coitus — fact or fiction?" *Med Asp of Hum Sex* 21:22–26.

Master, W. H., Johnson, V. E. 1966. *Human sexual response.* pp. 35, 174. Boston: Little & Brown.

Mayou, R. 1978. "Psychological aspects of ischaemic heart disease." *The Practitioner* 220:396–400.

____, Williamson, B., Foster, A. 1976. "Attitudes and advice after myocardial infarction." *Brit Med J* 1:1577–79.

____, Foster, A., Williamson, B. 1978. "The psychological and social effects of myocardial infarction on wives." *Brit Med J* 1:699–701.

McLane, M., Krop, H., Mehta, J. 1980. "Psychosexual adjustment and counseling after myocardial infarction." *Ann of Int Med* 92:514–19.

Mehta, J., Krop, H. 1979. "The effect of myocardial infarction on sexual functioning." *Sexuality & Disability* 2:115–21.

Miller, N. H., Gossard, D., Taylor, C. B. 1984. "Advice to resume sexual activity after myocardial infarction." *Circulation* 70 (Supp II):134.

Myers, A., Dewar, H. A. 1975. "Circumstances attending 100 sudden deaths from coronary artery disease with coroner's necropsies." *Brit Heart J* 37:1133–43.

Nalbantgil, I., Yigitbasi, O., Kiliccioglu, B. 1976. "Sudden death in sexual activity." *Amer Heart J* 91:405–06.

Nemec, E.D., Mansfield, L., Kennedy, J. W. 1976. "Heart rate and blood pressure responses during sexual activity in normal males." *Amer Heart J* 92:274–77.

Okoniewski, G. A. 1979. "Sexual activity following myocardial infarction." *Cardiovasc Nurs* 15:1–4.

Papadopoulos, C. 1978. "A survey of sexual activity after myocardial infarction." *Cardiovasc Med* 3:821–26.

____. 1980. "Cardiovascular drugs and sexuality." *Arch Intern Med* 140:1341–45.

____, Beaumont, C., Shelley, S. I. et al. 1983. "Myocardial infarction and sexual activity of the female patient." *Arch Intern Med* 143:1528–30.

____, Larrimore, P., Cardin, S. et al. 1980. "Sexual concerns and needs of the postcoronary patient's wife." *Arch Intern Med* 140:38–41.

Sanderson, M. O., Held, J. P., Bohlen, J. G. 1982. "Heart rate during masturbation." *J Cardiac Rehab* 2:542–46.

Scalzi, C. C. 1982. "Sexual counseling and sexual therapy for patients after myocardial infarction." *Cardiovasc Nurs* 18:13–17.

____, Loya, F., Golden, J. S. 1977. "Sexual therapy of patients with cardiovascular disease." *West J Med* 126:237–44.

Sjogren, K., Fugl-Meyer, A. R. 1983. "Some factors influencing quality of sexual life after myocardial infarction." *Int Rehab Med* 5:197–201.

Skelton, M., Dominian, J. 1973. "Psychological stress in wives of patients with myocardial infarction." *Brit Med J* 2:101–03.

Stein, R. A. 1977. "The effect of exercise training on heart rate during coitus in the post myocardial infarction patient." *Circulation* 55:738–40.

____. 1984. "Sexual dysfunction and the patient with coronary heart disease." *Arch Intern Med* 144:1744.

Stern, M. J., Pascale, L., Ackerman, A. 1977. "Life adjustment postmyocardial infarction." *Arch Intern Med* 137:1680–85.

Stern, T. A. 1985. "The management of depression and anxiety following myocardial infarction." *Mt. Sinai J of Med* 52:623–33.

Tofler, G. H., Stone, P. H., Muller, J. E. et al. 1987. "Effects of gender and race on prognosis after myocardial infarction: Adverse prognosis for women, particularly black women." *JACC* 3:473–82.

Tuttle, W. B., Cook, W. L., Fitch, E. 1964. "Sexual behavior in post-myocardial patients." *Am J Cardiol* (Abstract) 13:140.

Ueno, M. 1963. "The so-called coition death." *Jap J of Leg Med* 127:333–40.

Wagner, N. 1975. "Sexual activity and the cardiac patient." In *Human sexuality: A health practitioner's text,* edited by R. Green. Baltimore: Williams & Wilkins.

Watts, R. J. 1976. "Sexuality and the middle-aged cardiac patient." *Nurs Clin North Am* 11:349–59.

Wenger, N. K. 1981. *Rehabilitation of the patient with symptomatic coronary atherosclerotic heart disease.* Dallas: American Heart Association.

Wiklund, I., Sanne, H., Elmfeldt, D. et al. 1984. "Emotional reaction, health preoccupation and sexual activity two months after a myocardial infarction." *Scand J Rehab Med* 16:47–56.

Wishnie, H. A., Hackett, T. P., Cassem, N. A. 1971. "Psychological hazards of convalescence following myocardial infarction." *JAMA* 215:1292–96.

2
Sex and the Non-coronary Cardiac Patient

Although coronary artery disease is the most commonly encountered cardiac condition, other forms of heart disease also present medical and psychosocial problems. Little attention has been paid to the latter and especially the sexuality of these patients. Congenital heart disease, acquired valvular conditions, cardiomyopathies, and such consequences of heart disease as heart failure and arrhythmias create particular sexual concerns. An increasing population with permanent pacemakers also demands attention.

CONGENITAL HEART DISEASE

An estimated 28,000 infants are born annually with congenital heart disease (approximately 0.8 percent of all births). While about half of these infants die within the first year, health professionals may encounter adults with congenital heart disease because years of intense diagnostic and therapeutic efforts have resulted in the survival of increasing numbers of adolescents and adults with congenital defects of the heart. Thus, this disease may be represented not only by anomalies with a natural tendency for long survival, but also by those for which palliative or corrective surgery has been used. Appropriate long-term management requires an understanding of both the preoperative anomaly and the effects of surgical repair (Perloff 1979).

Adults with congenital heart disease may present sexual problems and dysfunction. However, statistical data are unavailable.

These patients need accurate diagnostic and functional evaluation by cardiologists to determine the type of heart disease, whether cyanotic or acyanotic, the presence of a particular valvular or septal defect, the type of shunting, and the presence of other extra-cardiac defects or pulmonary hypertension.

The impact on the sexual function of these patients may be due to their physical capacity and response to exercise, the presence of arrhythmias, the effects of medications, and the psychological effect of the long-term medical and/or the surgical care they may have required. Associated somatic congenital defects and physical appearance may affect the self-esteem of the patient and his or her interest in sexual activity.

In female teenagers with persistent cyanosis, sexual maturation is delayed, often for one to two years beyond the age at which it occurs among their peers. Menarche may be followed for several years by irregular menses. Most adults with congenital heart defects are able to establish a successful new family unit and have children with normal hearts. Women with Eisenmenger's syndrome are an exception; for them pregnancy is contraindicated. Certain rare cardiac syndromes have major effects on reproductive ability (Neill 1987).

Certain congenital defects, which are hemodynamically non-significant may not interfere with interpersonal and sexual relations. Patients with hemodynamic lesions who are successfully operated upon definitely improve functionally. Post-operative care should include exercise testing for proper evaluation.

Rehabilitation programs based on appropriate exercise prescriptions for reconditioning, combined with psychological counseling, will have a positive impact on the physical, emotional, and sexual rehabilitation of the patient.

ACQUIRED VALVULAR HEART DISEASE

The consequences of stenosis or regurgitation of the heart valves may be considered in relation to their direct effects on the cardiac chamber that must compensate for the valvular lesion (hypertrophy or dilatation) and their effects on intravascular pressures and blood flow. When a semilunar valve of the heart (aortic or pulmonic) is stenotic or regurgitant or when an atrio-ventricular valve (mitral or tricuspid) is regurgitant, the primary burden is placed upon the adjacent ventricle. Secondary effects develop in the arterial pressure in aortic valve disease. When the mitral or tricuspid valve is stenotic, there is a burden placed on the atrium, with secondary effects on the adjacent venous bed. The patient may exhibit no symptoms when the lesions are hemodynamically non-significant or may develop one or more of the following symptoms: shortness of breath, weakness, fatigue, syncope, chest pain, arrhythmias, and palpitations.

The physical limitations may affect the patient's sexual function, and this may be further complicated by anxiety, fear, and other psychological problems, such as depression. Furthermore, cardiovascular medications used to alleviate the above symptoms may lead to sexual side effects and dysfunction.

Rehabilitation of these patients should be based on accurate diagnosis and optimal medical management or, whenever indicated, surgical repair. Their evaluation, particularly in regard to their exercise tolerance and appearance of any arrhythmias with exertion, is vital. Twenty-four-hour Holter monitor recording of the electrocardiogram, including the period of sexual activity, will provide information for further adjustment of treatment.

For the patient with shortness of breath, a position of propping the chest and head up with pillows or sitting in an armchair during coitus should be recommended. The patient who had surgery with valve prosthesis and is on anticoagulants should be advised as to the risk of hematomas during very active sexual activity.

MITRAL VALVE PROLAPSE

Mitral valve prolapse should receive particular consideration due to its high incidence, especially among young sexually active individuals. The incidence has been reported to be 6 to 17 percent among otherwise healthy individuals (Markiewicz et al. 1976; Procacci et al. 1976; Darsee et al. 1979). However, some may exhibit a broad spectrum of symptoms that include atypical chest pains, weakness, fatigue, palpitations, lightheadedness, and shortness of breath. Instances of syncope have been reported. Other complications such as stroke, progressive mitral regurgitation, infective endocarditis, and sudden death may occur.

Typical auscultatory findings and echocardiography are important for the diagnosis, but exercise testing and Holter monitor recording provide information in regard to arrhythmias, which are common with this condition. In one series of 24 patients (Winkle et al. 1975) 50 percent of the patients had frequent premature ventricular beats and five patients in this group had ventricular tachycardia. Sixty-two percent had atrial premature beats, with seven patients presenting supraventricular tachycardia.

Anxiety often develops in these individuals, particularly when symptoms appear in conjunction with sexual activity, which may lead to dysfunction. Beta-blockers have been useful in controlling the symptoms, but they should be used with caution, especially in male patients, because of their effect on potency.

CARDIOMYOPATHIES

These conditions have been of various etiologies and have been classified into dilated (congestive), hypertrophic, and restrictive types. The symptoms of cardiomyopathy include weakness, fatigue and dyspnea upon exertion. Chest pain, though not common, may also occur. Palpitations are frequent.

In the congestive cardiomyopathies, there is systolic pump failure and dilatation of the left ventricle. The patient develops symptoms of congestive heart failure and has arrhythmias or conduction abnormalities. Management with digitalis, diuretics, and vasodilators and, when necessary, anti-arrhythmics may improve the functional capacity of the patients. Often, however, the long-term incapacitation of the patients makes them lose interest in sexual activity. The underlying cause of the cardiomyopathy, which may be infective, metabolic, nutritional, neuromuscular, systemic, or toxic may directly contribute to the patient's dysfunction.

In patients with alcoholic cardiomyopathy, beyond the hemodynamic effects of heart disease, one should consider the effects of alcohol itself on the sexual function. Acute alcohol intoxication may impede sexual performance. It may inhibit erection, ejaculation, and orgasm (Hammond 1984; Smith 1985). Chronic alcohol use causes gonadal and liver damage that has hormonal effects. Polyneuropathy may also appear. Hypogonadism, reduced sperm count, reduced testosterone levels, and increased estrogen and prolactin levels are noted in men. Body hair is diminished and gynecomastia, decreased libido, and impotence develop. In women, decreased fertility, amenorrhea, premature ovarian failure, and reduction in breast size can occur. Abstention from alcohol is vital for the rehabilitation of these patients, in addition to psychological and pharmacological approaches.

In hypertrophic cardiomyopathy the pump function of the heart is usually maintained until late in the disease, but the patient has symptoms of angina, dyspnea, and syncope, which may interfere with his or her sexual performance.

Beta-blockers, calcium blockers and, if unsuccessful, cardiac surgery may be indicated to improve the functional capacity of the heart.

HEART FAILURE

As a pump the heart is remarkable, not only for its capacity to rapidly adjust to metabolic needs and varying loads, but also for its durability. It is, however, vulnerable to a wide group of congenital, metabolic, inflammatory, and degenerative disorders that affect the muscular wall, its linings, its valves, and the coronary arteries. When the heart is unable to match its output to the metabolic needs of the body, physiological heart failure has developed. Clinically, heart failure refers to a distinctive group of symptoms and signs that appear in a patient with underlying cardiac disorder. Respiratory discomfort or distress, fatigue, and weakness dominate the symptoms of left heart failure. They vary with position, stress, and activity. Depending on the underlying cause, surgical or medical management of the patient may alleviate the symptoms and improve functional capacity. The management should center on identification and treatment of both the precipitating cause and the underlying cardiac abnormality. Restriction of fluid and sodium intake, use of digitalis, diuretics, and peripheral vasodilators will provide medical support and improvement. Sexual activity is usually prohibited in patients with poorly controlled congestive heart failure, since this may easily lead to aggravation of the condition and even pulmonary edema. Alternate expressions of sexual feelings and affection may be encouraged (caressing, hugging, and kissing). Compensated patients may be permitted to resume sexual activity, but coital positions to avoid pulmonary congestion, such as lying propped up with pillows or sitting up in a chair, should be advised for such patients.

CARDIAC ARRHYTHMIAS

In patients who have chronic paroxysmal atrial arrhythmias, the impact on sexual activity, like other types of physical activity, should be considered. When associated with underlying heart disease, they must be viewed in the context of the underlying cause and the symptoms that may appear in association with the heart disease. At other times people present atrial arrhythmias of unknown etiology or without evidence of detectable heart disease. Premature atrial beats or attacks of paroxysmal atrial tachycardia may be precipitated by effort or emotion, including sexual activity. Appearance of these arrhythmias may cause fear and concern, which can lead to sexual dysfunction. The patient may complain of palpitations, chest discomfort, dizziness, lightheadedness, or syncope. Detection, diagnosis, and evaluation of the arrhythmia may be made by electrocardiograms, Holter monitor recording, and exercise testing. Prophylactic antiarrhythmic treatment can control these arrhythmias. Medications may be used on a regular basis if the arrhythmias occur frequently. Recently termination of paroxysms of arrhythmias with single doses of antiarrhythmics has been reported in the literature (Yeh et al. 1985; Benson et al. 1985).

Patients with chronic atrial fibrillation may remain symptom-free during coitus but may complain of palpitations if the ventricular rate is not well controlled with medications. Treatment for any cardiac incapacity during sexual activity in patients with sustained atrial flutter or fibrillation should be directed toward the underlying condition and optimal control of the ventricular rate (Regestein and Horn 1978).

Ventricular arrhythmias may lead to palpitations, lightheadedness, and dizziness, but sustained ventricular tachycardia may lead to syncope and/or ventricular fibrillation and death. Careful clinical observation and evaluation of ventricular arrhythmias is needed. Stressful psychological factors should be determined, since it is known that even in the absence of heart disease they may provoke lethal arrhythmias (Lown et al. 1976). Certain sexual situations, such as extramarital sex, may be more likely to provoke arrhythmic episodes than others (Marmor and Kert 1958; Johnston and Fletcher 1979). Some feel that illicit sex, often with a casual acquaintance and especially after drinks and a heavy meal, is more likely to be associated with sudden death, presumably due to ventricular fibrillation, than sex under more familiar circumstances (Massie et al. 1969; Ueno 1963). Avoidance of such precipitating factors and appropriate anti-arrhythmic therapy may lead to control of such arrhythmias. If the patient's history and subsequent test with Holter monitor recording indicate no advanced grades of ventricular arrhythmia, the physician may advise the patient against restriction of normal sexual activity.

Effective reassurance of the patient with arrhythmias will require a trusting alliance between physician and patient and a conscious effort by the physician to specifically discuss sexual behavior, with the spouse present (Regestein and Horn 1978). The spouse or sexual partner may be more anxious than the patient and may feel guilty about making his or her sexual needs known. Considerable effort may be needed to overcome fears of sexual activity. If the physician avoids this topic he or she may aggravate the concerns and anxiety of the couple living with cardiac arrhythmia. The vast majority of patients subject to arrhythmia should be able to enjoy sexual activity with no hesitation or fear and may be encouraged to do so. The rare individual in whom sexual activity precipitates or worsens an arrhythmia can be helped by medical management so that he or she, too, can enjoy a normal sex life.

Patients with congenital complete heart block are often able to tolerate sexual activity with no or minimal symptoms. Patients who suddenly, transiently, or permanently develop complete heart block may develop dizziness or syncope. A unique case of complete heart block with "coital" convulsions has been described (Kelly 1977). On several occasions, a 55-year-old man had an acute onset of seizures occurring during the immediate post-orgasmic phase of sexual intercourse. When he was admitted to the hospital for evaluation, the electrocardiogram showed prolonged P-R interval, right bundle branch block, and right posterior hemi-block, but during a similar sudden episode of loss of consciousness, complete heart block with a ventricular rate of 28/minute was noted. The seizure disorder was corrected with the implantation of a permanent epicardial pacemaker.

PATIENTS WITH PERMANENT PACEMAKERS

More than 100,000 permanent pacemakers are implanted annually. Since many of these patients are not elderly and are still sexually active, sexual concerns often develop. One is the disfigurement because of the insertion of the generator. Others are that the motion or excessive activity during sexual relations may hurt the site of the operation and the generator and may interfere with its function. Patients are also concerned about the impact of certain sexual positions on the generator and its potential damage.

Beyond these concerns, real problems that may affect sexual activity appear, if the place of implantation of the pacemaker generator and the scarring around the area of the incision interfere and cause some limitation of movement of the shoulder or arm. Furthermore, myopotentials may cause interference with the function of certain pacemakers. The insertion of a permanent pacemaker for certain bradyarrhythmias may not eliminate the recurrence of atrial or ventricular arrhythmias, which may still develop and lead to symptoms during sexual activity. Also problems from the underlying disease, such as angina pectoris and congestive heart failure, may still exist and interfere with the proper performance of the patient.

Proper evaluation of the patient should include sexual history and the level of previous sexual activity before implantation of the pacemaker. The benefits and the potential complications should be explained. Addressing the patient's sexual concerns before and after the implantation may alleviate the fears and anxiety of the patient and spouse. It is best to wait two weeks after implantation for the wound to heal completely and the intracardiac catheter electrode to be well "fixed," before resuming sexual activity. The patient should be advised against any position that could cause tension on the electrode and should be instructed to communicate to the physician any symptoms that develop during sexual activity. The recent availability of atrio-ventricular sequential pacemakers and of ones that are rate responsive to activity provide a new dimension to improved functional capacity of patients.

BIBLIOGRAPHY

Benson, D. W., Dunnigan, A., Green, T. P. et al. 1985. "Periodic Procainamide for paroxysmal tachycardia." *Circulation* 72:147–52.

Darsee, J. R., Mikolich, J. R., Nicoloff, N. B. et al. 1979. "Prevalence of mitral valve prolapse in presumably healthy young men." *Circulation* 59:619–22.

Hammond, D. C. 1984. "Alcohol: An impediment to erection and orgasm." *Med Asp of Hum Sex* 6:191–95.

Johnston, B. L., Fletcher, G. F. 1979. "Dynamic electrocardiographic recording during sexual activity in recent post-myocardial infarction and revascularization patients." *Am Heart J* 98:736–41.

Kelly, J. R. 1977. "Coital (cardiac) convulsions: Case report of a unique presentation of complete heart block." *J Fam Prac* 4:1073–75.

Lown, B., Tempte, J. V., Reich, P. et al. 1976. "The basis for recurring ventricular fibrillation in the absence of coronary heart disease and its management." *N Engl J Med* 294:623–29.

Markiewicz, W., Stoner, J., London, E. et al. 1976. "Mitral valve prolapse in one hundred presumably healthy young females." *Circulation* 53:464–73.

Marmor, J., Kert, M. J. 1958. "Paroxysmal ventricular tachycardia." *Calif Med* 88:325–29.

Massie, E., Rose, E. F., Rupp, J. C. et al. 1969. "Viewpoints: Sudden death during coitus — fact or fiction?" *Med Asp of Hum Sex* 3:22–26.

Neill, C. A. 1987. "Quality of life issues in the adult with congenital heart disease: The next generation." *Quality of Life and Cardiovascular Care* 3:57–60.

Perloff, J. K. 1979. "Congenital Heart Disease." In *Textbook of Medicine*, edited by P. B. Beeson, W. McDermott and J. B. Wyngaarden. Philadelphia: W. B. Saunders.

Procacci, P., Savaran, S. V., Schreiter, S. L. et al. 1976. "Prevalence of clinical mitral valve prolapse in 1169 young women." *N Engl J Med* 294: 1086–88.

Regestein, Q. R., Horn, H. R. 1978. "Coitus in patients with cardiac arrhythmias." *Med Asp of Hum Sex* 12:108–21.

Smith, J. W. 1985. "Sexual function in patients with chronic viral hepatitis and alcoholic cirrhosis." *Med Asp of Hum Sex* 7:197–98.

Ueno, M. 1963. "The so-called coition death." *Jap J Legal Med* 17:333–40.

Winkle, R. A., Lopes, M. G., Fitzgerald, J. W. et al. 1975. "Arrhythmias in patients with mitral valve prolapse." *Circulation* 52:73–81.

Yeh, S. J., Lin, F. C., Chou, Y. Y. et al. 1985. "Termination of paroxysmal supraventricular tachycardia with a single oral dose of Diltiazem and Propranolol." *Circulation* 71:104–09.

3
Quality of Life and Sexual Activity after Cardiac Surgery

During the past three decades, cardiac surgery has developed rapidly and much interest has often been directed to the technical challenges and survival statistics. Slowly a need developed to find out more about the quality of life of patients who have undergone heart surgery and to learn more about not only alleviation of symptoms, but return to useful employment and social and recreational activities. However, although there is much information in the literature about work status after heart surgery, less emphasis has been given to the psychosocial status and even less to the sexual activity of the patients.

For many patients a surgical operation is a major crisis, the anticipation and consequences of which evoke serious psychologic disorders, quite apart from the gravity of the illness or the extent of the surgery (Hackett and Weisman 1960). Patients with progressive or incapacitating ailments may undergo heroic surgical measures and recover promptly, while others with trivial complaints sometimes have a prolonged convalescence or a refractory hospital course following a relatively minor operation. Cardiac surgery creates an even stronger climate of fear and anxiety and at the same time greater expectations for recovery and a useful and enjoyable life. A "good" surgical result is not a panacea. Patients may "improve," but they are not truly cured of their cardiac disability. Many patients improve dramatically, but a smaller percentage may experience little or no improvement. In fact, only a small proportion of patients, those with corrected congenital defects, can be thought to be totally rehabilitated (Heller et al. 1974).

Following an operation, all patients face a period of enforced inactivity and dependent care. When they are expected to return to "normal life," for example, resume work, family, and general social functioning, this may be complicated by employer bias, the patient's and the spouse's fear of sexual or other exertion, and the adjustment to a large, visible surgical scar (Heller et al. 1974). Some patients will be faced with recurrent medical problems such as hepatitis, phlebitis, arrhythmia, embolization, and even the need for re-operation. Such sequelae are especially devastating for a patient who has just overcome the surgical ordeal. Many patients may also require cardiac medications and must observe salt, caloric, and tobacco restrictions.

Still, many patients present sexual interests, get married, and at times pregnant after congenital, valvular, and coronary artery surgery (Perloff 1973; Garson et al. 1979; Lutz et al. 1978; Reece et al. 1986; Chestnut et al. 1986).

SURGERY FOR VALVULAR AND
CONGENITAL HEART DISEASE

In a study of 792 patients (Frank et al. 1972) the adjustment to cardiac surgery was surveyed by means of a questionnaire. Sixty percent of the total number of respondents were women. Sixty-five percent had open heart surgery. Most of the patients had valvular disease and 14 percent had congenital heart disease. The results of the study generally showed positive medical, social, and emotional status following the surgery, with nearly all patients feeling "glad" they had elected to have surgery. The authors stated that the virtual unanimity is striking, considering that patients experienced pain, frequent delirium, sometimes poor surgical results, and even re-operation. Frank and colleagues believed that the apparent reason for this positive concensus, even when poor physical results were obtained, was that patients believed that without surgery they would not have survived. Furthermore, having subjected themselves to a more stressful, life threatening and costly operation, patients might tend to rationalize their decision to be the correct one. Psychological and psychiatric symptoms were common in the immediate post-operative period. While there was a general improvement in long-term psychological condition in most cases, 17 percent of their sample felt that psychological factors impeded their recovery, independently of medical status. While many patients made appreciable psychological gains by six months, others required a full year to attain the same level of improvement. They also concluded that an overprotective family, and a physician telling the patient what he or she should not do, and failing to specify what to do, could result in prolonged invalidism and failure to resume appropriate independent activity. When the authors studied the psychological outcome after surgery and reviewed "pleasure in life," job performance, mood, nervousness, family and sexual relations, 49 percent of the patients showed improvement of sexual activity at 12 months, but this area exhibited less improvement than all the others. The sexual activity was reported as unchanged by 42 percent and worse by 9 percent of the patients. It appeared that sexual activity was the least improved area of functioning, with patients apparently reluctant to engage in that activity. The authors felt that more extensive patient and family education by physicians, for which their study strongly suggested a general need, may be particularly indicated in the sexual area.

In the study of Heller and his group (1974) 70 of 142 survivors of open heart surgery returned for follow-up interviews one year after the operation. Most of them had valvular surgery and 11 percent had repair of congenital defects. Over 90 percent of the patients showed improvement in the physical condition compared with preoperative evaluations. However, general psychological adjustment declined after the operation, with significant psychological hindrances to recovery occurring in approximately one-third of the patients. These patients were generally maladjusted, showing high levels of anxiety, depression, and somatic preoccupation. They tended to think poorly of themselves and although generally socially withdrawn, they sought excessive help from those with whom they were involved. Their sexual function was impaired and they showed a marked tendency to blame others for their misfortunes. Poor preoperative psychological adjustment was more strongly associated with hindrances than was the actual physical outcome. Low preoperative desire for surgery was also ominous.

A study from the United Kingdom (Ross et al. 1978) presented data based on repeat interviews with 100 male and 100 female patients who had undergone open heart surgery between 1973 and 1974. Most of them had single or multiple valve replacements, and 9 percent of the patients were operated on for congenital heart disease and 7 percent for coronary artery bypass grafts. The questionnaire elicited information on physical activity, employment, dependence on others, leisure activities, mood, and sexual relationships. The results showed that 20 months after the operation, 68 percent of the survivors did not limit normal activity compared with a preoperative figure of 12 percent and that there had been a corresponding pattern in return to useful employment. Decreased dependence on others was readily identified as a significant gain for 73 percent of patients at the eight-month followup. Throughout the subsequent year, the favorable trends in employment statistics, use of leisure time, mood, and sexual relationships pointed to an overall improvement in the quality of life for the majority of patients. One hundred thirty-six married patients in the group were questioned during the first interview to what extent sexual relationships had been affected by the patient's ill health. Eighty-five (63 percent) said there had been deterioration, while 51 (37 percent) had experienced no change. Post-operative improvement was slow, in many cases due to fear of exertion and lack of confidence. Another reason given for this slow progress was the unfamiliar sound of a prosthetic valve. By 20 months after surgery, 42 (31 percent) of the patients said that sexual relationships had improved since the operation.

A survey of adults and adolescents after repair of the tetralogy of Fallot (Garson et al. 1979) attempted to provide follow-up data for physicians concerned with their care. This congenital anomaly consists of right ventricular hypertrophy, right ventricular outflow obstruction, a large ventricular septal defect, and overriding of the interventricular septum by the root of the aorta. The study was based on patients who had intracardiac repair of the defects at a median age of 9.7 years. Of the survivors who were contacted several years later (at the median age of 22.2 years), 95 responded to a questionnaire. Eighty-four denied symptoms, 44 had attended college, and all were employed. Twenty-eight (18 men and 10 women) had married. Two marriages ended in divorce. No patient reported having infertility. None of the female patients or the wives of the male patients had miscarriages. None of the 26 progeny had congenital heart disease.

Patients with congenital heart disease who undergo successful complete repair should be able to have normal employment status and function socially and sexually as normal individuals once any psychological hindrances that may have developed are resolved.

CORONARY ARTERY BYPASS GRAFT SURGERY

More than 200,000 coronary artery bypass graft (CABG) operations are performed every year (American Heart Association 1988). Initially many reports concentrated on the relief of angina and on the employment status of the patients after surgery. Review articles (Oberman et al. 1982; Rahimtoola 1982; Davidson 1983) summarized previous such studies. Though emphasis has lately been put on the quality of life of coronary artery bypass patients, little information has been gathered about their sexual activity.

Quality of life is a complex value concept used to evaluate the desire to lead a particular lifestyle and includes that which makes life worthwhile. In a review of the quality of life after coronary artery bypass surgery (Smith 1985), quality of life components considered were cardiac symptoms, hospitalizations, reduction in medications, prevention of infarction, employment status, and recreational activity. In prospective randomized studies (Rahimtoola 1982) CABG has reduced symptoms in 76 to 90 percent of patients; 33 to 55 percent of patients became asymptomatic and 5 to 6 percent deteriorated. Subsequent hospitalizations were significantly fewer for surgically treated patients with unstable or more severe chronic stable angina than for those treated medically (Smith 1985). The need for medications was reduced, but coronary bypass surgery had no clear benefit over medical therapy in the prevention of infarction or development of heart failure symptoms. Because angina is relieved and functional capacity improved in the majority of patients after coronary bypass surgery, it was initially believed that the surgery would allow previously disabled patients to return to the work force. This has not generally been the case and the correlation between functional improvement and the return to work is poor. A number of investigators whose studies were summarized by Smith (1985) have examined the influence of various biomedical and non-medical factors that might modify the effect of coronary bypass surgery on post-operative employment status. None of the preoperative clinical and angiographic indicators of severity of coronary artery disease influenced the post-operative employment rate. The preoperative factors determining post-operative employment are socioeconomic, for example, whether working before surgery and type of occupation. Smith and his group (1982) found no significant relationship between the level of post-operative recreational activity and post-operative employment for any job category. The improvement in non-work physical activity was similar in both working and non-working men. Eighty-four percent of non-working and 88 percent of working men reported improved or unchanged levels of physical activity after surgery. This lack of correlation between non-work physical activity and post-operative employment re-emphasizes the importance of the non-medical factors in influencing the return to work.

In a study of 318 patients with an average age of 54.4 years Jenkins and colleagues (1983) reviewed the physical, psychological, social and economic outcomes six months after coronary artery bypass surgery. Angina was completely relieved for 69 to 85 percent of persons. Seventy-five percent of previously employed persons had returned to work. Twenty percent of those unemployed at the time of operation resumed work. The preoperative expectation of a patient to return to work was highly predictive of vocational outcome. By six months after surgery the great majority of patients appeared to have experienced substantial medical benefits, relief of physical and related psychological symptoms, restored physical and social function, the ability to return to work, and an enhanced quality of life.

A comprehensive review article (Kinchla and Weiss 1985) surveyed many studies of the psychologic and social outcomes of coronary artery bypass surgery. In regard to the employment status of the patients, they found tremendous variability of figures in various studies. The average of studies reporting patients who worked before and after surgery was 76 percent, and for those who did not work before surgery but resumed employment afterward, it was 27.6 percent. Medical status before and after surgery was generally correlated with return to work following CABG. Angina and fatigue appear to be the most frequently reported medical symptoms associated with work status. Socioeconomic levels, occupational level, family income, and educational status were found to be positively correlated with overall employment. Type A personality patients exhibited poorer social and emotional adjustment than Type B individuals (Zyzanski et al. 1981), but Type A patients were more often employed than Type B after surgery (Gundle et al. 1980).

In a study of early appraisal of coronary revascularization on quality of life (Penckofer and Holm 1984), two groups, one of 17 patients 3 to 5 months after surgery and another of 17 patients 6 to 8 months after surgery, were asked to evaluate themselves in relation to past, present, and future life satisfaction. The findings indicated that following CABG there were measurable improvements in the quality of life early in the recovery period. As early as three to five months postoperatively, patients reported higher levels of life satisfaction. Although patients in this period did not perceive their present and past quality of life as significantly different, they did project the future as being significantly better than the past. Patients further along in the recovery process, six to eight months, also experienced increased levels of satisfaction. Moreover, they saw their present and future quality of life as superior to the past. The difference between the groups in the assessment of present life satisfaction may be related to the effects of time on the recovery process. The authors felt that the life satisfaction ratings given by the patients in the early months of recovery may have been affected by the limitations imposed by residual incisional pain. Both groups also reported greater satisfaction with family, social, and sexual life following surgery. Most of the patients stated that their dissatisfaction with sexual life prior to surgery was due to fear. Some reported that anginal pain interfered with the ability to have intercourse. Several of the spouses also reported fear of causing injury to their partner. After surgery patients stated that although initially afraid to have intercourse because of the chest incision, anginal pain was not experienced when sexual activity was resumed.

In the study by Jenkins and his group (1983) 80 percent of the patients reported, after surgery, receiving as much affection as they would like from the people with whom they lived, and 74 percent believed that the people closest to them really understood how they felt most or all of the time. Half of the patients reported that overall their surgery had affected their family by bringing them closer together, whereas only 3 percent thought that it had pulled them further apart. Half of the patients reported no post-operative change in the level of satisfaction with their sexual life, compared with one year before surgery. The remainder were equally divided between those reporting better or worse levels of satisfaction. For persons who now had less satisfaction, the most common attributed reasons were reductions in sexual desire and energy levels. Reports of increased sexual satisfaction were positively correlated with the level of marital happiness.

In a study on the return to work and quality of life after surgery for coronary artery disease (Westaby, Sapsford and Bentall 1979) reference to the sexual activity of their patients was made. They stated that surgery provided dramatic symptomatic relief in up to 90 percent of their patients. Of those wishing to engage in hobbies or sports, social activity, and sexual intercourse — but were restricted before the operation — about two-thirds could resume these activities afterward. They stated that after prolonged suffering from angina with restricted physical activity, avoidance of excitement, and abstinence from sexual intercourse, their patients showed a pronounced alteration in life-style. Ninety-six percent of patients who had been sexually active at the onset of symptoms were restricted by angina. After operation, 70 percent were restored to previous activity, though shortness of breath or hesitancy and concern on behalf of the partner remained as prohibiting factors.

Two studies that addressed the psychosocial outcome after coronary artery surgery also dealt with the sexual adjustment of the patients and revealed a negative impact. One study (Gundle et al. 1980) reported on interviews with 30 patients before and one to two years after surgery. Despite good physiologic outcome (as measured by treadmill and cardiac function) this sample was found to be functioning poorly. Eighty-three percent were unemployed and 57 percent were sexually impaired. Whereas 73 percent of the patients reported satisfactory sexual functioning before surgery, only 43 percent of the total group felt this way afterward. All patients participated in an active post-operative physical rehabilitation program. The authors felt that the lower employment rate was probably due to the lower socioeconomic status of their group of patients and the patients' damaged self-concept, especially in view of a prolonged period of symptoms prior to surgery. This damaged self-image was highly correlated with poor sexual functioning, particularly in males. The sexual function and followup were also associated with the duration of symptoms and the preoperative sexual status.

In a report based on 100 patients who underwent coronary artery surgery (Kornfeld et al. 1982) 54 patients had personal follow-up visits nine months post-operatively and were interviewed in regard to many aspects of their psychosocial behavior. The response to the questions on sexual activity revealed that before surgery 67 percent were sexually active at least once a week, 22 percent were less active, and 11 percent had no sexual activity. Nine months post-operatively, only 38 percent were sexually active at least once a week and 31 percent reported no sexual activity. Post-operative frequency of sexual activity correlated with preoperative cardiac impairment, return to work, and pre- and post-operative Type A personality ratings. When information was obtained an average of three and one-half years after surgery, 44 percent stated that sexual satisfaction was better than before surgery. However, sexual adjustment and satisfaction improved the least in comparison to other parameters of quality of life, including general pleasure, anxiety, depression, job satisfaction, and family relations.

Data from four previously published studies of chronic angina and bypass surgery that evaluated various clinical features (Rahimtoola 1982) showed that 50 percent of the patients had no symptoms during sexual activity and of the rest, 16 percent had angina. In one of these studies, the Veterans Administration Cooperative Study (Peduzzi and Hultgren 1979), the impairment of sexual activity and the associated angina were relative to whether all, some, or none of the vein grafts had remained patent after surgery. The impairment of sexual activity varied from 29 to 52 percent and the incidence of associated angina from 8 to 36 percent.

Efforts to obtain specific information about the sexual activity after CABG have been made based on a small series of patients. In a study of the sexual activity in exercising patients after myocardial infarction and revascularization (Johnston et al. 1978), 19 men who had CABG responded in a mean of 23 months after surgery. The average age was 51.6 years. These patients resumed sexual activity sooner than the myocardial infarction patients (5.7 weeks vs. 9.4 weeks). There was no apparent difference in frequency of sexual activity before and after the revascularization. Twenty-one percent of the group experienced angina pectoris associated with sexual intercourse.

Data were also reported from 19 patients (5 female and 14 male), who underwent surgery in 1977 (Thurer 1981). The mean age was 53.5 years. All patients were evaluated in the hospital one or two days before surgery and approximately four months later in their homes. The patients' sexual adjustment had worsened with perceived symptoms of heart disease but did not improve following surgery. It was found that 42 percent of patients reported worsened sexual adjustment after surgery (compared with three months before surgery), 26 percent reported improvement, and 31 percent reported no change. Two-thirds of patients reported receiving no counseling, suggestions, or information regarding sexual activity. The patients showed a significant improvement in their physical condition. Most were relieved of angina following the operation, felt substantially more vigorous, but did not rebound sexually. The author felt that the fact that sexual functioning did not improve following successful surgery may be due to insufficient time allowed for rehabilitation (four months). We believe that this is highly probable since in other studies (Kornfeld et al. 1982) improvement of post-operative sexual functioning occurred with time.

The effects of CABG on female patients were reported (Althof, Coffman and Levine 1984) based on interviews with 17 women who underwent surgery. Four time periods were examined: prior to and after the onset of cardiac symptoms, four months and one year after CABG. The patients were operated on between 1980 and 1982. The mean age was 59.2 years. Seventy-five percent were married. The frequency of intercourse before surgery was more than once a week in 12 percent (two patients) and less than once a week in 35 percent (six patients). Fifty-three percent (nine patients) had no sexual activity. The same pattern was observed four months post-operatively, but three of the inactive patients resumed sexual activity, though not frequently, one year after surgery. Approximately half of the patients had no sexual desire prior to surgery and this decreased to 35 percent one year after CABG. It was interesting that none of the 17 women reported feeling sexually undesirable, either pre- or post-operatively. While they complained about surgical scar itching and pain, they denied feeling less attractive or disfigured by the scar. After surgery, sexual concerns had a low priority for these 17 patients. When specifically asked about post-surgical sexual concerns, only three inquired about resuming sexual activity. All patients denied fears of harming themselves with such activity but reported their husband's fears of harming them. At four months and one year post-operatively, no one expressed sexual concerns. In this study, women with high and low pre-illness sexual activity and desire levels had different sexual adaptations during the year after surgery. The sexual component that was most vulnerable to disruption was desire. The women with the highest desire and intercourse frequency were the most adversely affected by cardiac symptoms and surgery. The women did not express sexual fears such as sudden death during intercourse and performance anxiety. Several of them maintained that their partners were very worried about the surgery. They sought, however, to protect them from the interviewers taking the stance of not wanting to place an additional burden on them. A few of these women had been sexually inactive for a lengthy period and saw no need to interview their partners on that subject. The authors sensed a fear that an interview might cause their husbands to resume making sexual demands.

Any individual's adaptation is influenced by important events, such as illness and/or surgery as well as the partner's adaptation to that event. Both partners' idiosyncratic responses interact to produce changes in the couple's sexual equilibrium. Most post-CABG patients and their partners find sexual behavior reassuring. It facilitates self-esteem, provides hope by promising a return to a normal functioning level, and is an affirmation of the bond between them. However, sexual behavior is not important to all individuals after CABG. Some see the surgery as an excuse for retreating from marital duties.

We recently studied 134 patients who had coronary bypass surgery in 1982 and 1983 (Papadopoulos et al. 1986) by person-to-person interviews, based on a structured questionnaire. We focused on the effect of CABG on the various aspects of the sexual life of these patients. The group consisted of 102 males and 32 females. The mean age was 59 years. Seventy-four patients were working prior to surgery and 58 post-operatively returned to work at various times. Ninety-two patients in the group (68.6 percent) were sexually active before the surgery. The main reasons for sexual inactivity of the rest were lack of desire, lack of a partner, previous myocardial infarction or cardiac symptoms, and impotence. Of the 92 patients who were sexually active before the CABG, 84 (91 percent) resumed sexual activity, including coitus. The average time of resumption of sexual activity was 7.8 weeks and the overall frequency of sexual activity decreased from 6.2 to 4.8 times per month after the surgery. Sexual dissatisfaction prior to surgery was a negative factor, while return to work, in the group that was previously working, had a positive effect on resuming sexual activity. Seventeen percent of patients who were sexually active before CABG expressed fear of resuming sexual activity. They were afraid of a heart attack or chest pain, "hurting" the chest incision, or dying during coitus. The main reasons offered by the few who actually did not resume sexual activity were fear, lack of desire, and impotence. Of those who resumed sexual activity, 51 percent did not change the frequency, 10 percent increased it, and 39 percent decreased it. Among those who continued sexual activity after the surgery, 23 percent reported symptoms during coitus — mostly shortness of breath, fatigue, chest pain, or palpitations. Of the group that was sexually active post-operatively, 12 percent said that the quality of sex was better, 17 percent worse, and 71 percent the same, while 58 percent stated that the overall quality of life was better, 10 percent that it was worse, and 32 percent that it was the same. The emotional relationship became closer for those who resumed sexual activity in comparison to those in the group who did not resume or were sexually inactive even before the CABG.

Overall it appeared that a higher percentage of the previously sexually active patients resumed sexual activity after CABG than after myocardial infarction and they had less fear of resumption. There were also more patients increasing and fewer patients decreasing the frequency of sexual activity after surgery than after a heart attack (Papadopoulos 1978; Papadopoulos et al. 1983). This was also observed in another study from Israel (Levy et al. 1985).

Life adaptation after percutaneous transluminal coronary angioplasty, in comparison to coronary artery bypass grafting, was reviewed by Raft and associates (1985). Thirty-two patients who had undergone coronary angioplasty were compared with 15 patients who had coronary bypass surgery. The patients were matched for psychosocial, anatomic, and cardiac functions. Life adaptation was measured at 6 and 15 months. After six months the patients who had undergone angioplasty functioned better at work, in sexual performance and with their families. The improvements in work functioning continued at 15 months, but the difference in sexual and family domains became insignificant by that time.

The concerns and questions of wives of convalescent coronary artery bypass patients were investigated in a study of 30 women who were interviewed privately, in their homes, during the second or third week after their husbands were discharged from the hospital (Sikorski 1985). The main changes reported by the wives were increased fatigue and anxiety, better interpersonal relationship with the spouse, changes in daily life-style at home and outside the home, and differences of opinion with the spouse about convalescent expectations. An increased expression of feelings, a greater appreciation of each other, and a positive change in their husband's attitudes were reported. This finding might be anticipated in that the surgery is a procedure aimed at improving the quality of the patient's life. After an extended period of illness, many of the wives enjoy their husband's improved physical capabilities and reduction or absence of angina. The shared experience of the uncertainty of the surgery might also foster more openness and appreciation of each other. The majority of the wives had good knowledge of coronary risk factors but insufficient or only fair knowledge of their husband's medications and of the surgery and its relationship to coronary artery disease. The most frequently expressed concerns were future heart problems, death, prognosis, surgical success, behavioral fluctuations, and the potential for recurrence of arterial blockage. They also expressed concerns about their spouse's pain, posture, sleeping difficulties, and leg edema. Although the wives had knowledge of recommended activities, they lacked information about sexual activity. The majority believed that their husbands should not resume sexual activity during the second and third week of convalescence. They did not receive any formal guidelines at discharge. They were concerned about the safety, the time of resumption, and the welfare of their husbands during sexual activity.

CARDIAC TRANSPLANTATION

During the past several years, transplantation of the heart has emerged as a reliable, therapeutic alternative for end-stage congestive heart failure. Survival rates may reach 65 percent at 2 years (Schroeder and Hunt 1986). Most patients assume normal life-styles, but the medical literature is scant in regard to the psychiatric and the psychosocial impact of transplantation on the recipients. A recent report (Jones et al. 1988) addressed the psychological adjustment after cardiac transplantation. It was based on 32 men and 6 women with an average age of 38.8 years. There was significant reduction of anxiety in comparison to the state of the patient prior to the transplantation, and no depression was noted. There was improved satisfaction with life and the body image was enhanced as a result of improvements in physical-exercise tolerance and health. Over-exertion and causing damage to the new heart was "sometimes" a concern for 43 percent of the recipients. Only 21 percent worried about dying at some time after transplantation, compared to 100 percent of recipients having such fears prior to the operation. Twelve recipients, who were married and were followed for 12 months after transplantation, reported complete or nearly complete satisfaction with marriage. Their sexual activity and sexual satisfaction, however, was not reported. Other researchers (Lough and Shinn 1987) found that impotence and diminished libido are areas of considerable concern for many patients. A recent study (Harvison et al. 1988) of 51 heart recipients revealed that only 50 percent were either nearly or completely satisfied with their sexual life. Sexual activity had increased for 20 percent and decreased for another 29 percent of the patients.

As the number and survival time of heart transplant recipients continue to increase, their quality of life, including sexuality and child bearing, have become important issues (Kossoy, Herbert and Wentz 1988). Reproduction is possible for both male and female patients and has occurred after cardiac transplantation. Teratogenicity has not been reported, either with traditional immunosuppressive agents (prednisone, azathioprine) or with cyclosporine. The option of sterilization can be offered as a permanent procedure to patients who have completed their families or have no desire to have children. If sterilization of the patient or the spouse is not appropriate, the choice of contraception depends on balancing the desirability of pregnancy prevention against the potential risks of the contraceptive method (Kossoy, Herbert and Wentz 1988).

COUNSELING AND REHABILITATION

Counseling of the patient who undergoes cardiac surgery should start preoperatively and should address the physical, occupational, and psychosocial benefits and problems that may occur after surgery. The patient should know about the thoracotomy and sternotomy, the healing of the bone and wound, and be reassured about the potential discomfort that may linger for awhile. He or she should understand the relative rates of wound healing and the progressive improvement of exercise tolerance. The counselor, by developing a desire for re-employment and encouraging return to such a status, often assures the post-operative return of the patient to employment. Concerns about recreational and sexual activity after surgery should also be addressed and answered.

In the process of preparing patients for heart surgery, assisting them through recovery, and preparing them for discharge, the long-term effects of this experience on quality of life must be recognized (Penckofer and Holm 1984). Information on how patients perceive their quality of life during the immediate and later post-operative periods can assist physicians and nurses in the preparation of patients and their families for discharge. Furthermore, knowledge of life satisfaction levels following surgery offers an opportunity to appreciate the patients' perception of the situation and to assist them in setting short- and long-term goals.

Post-operatively, the treating staff should be alerted to symptoms of anxiety, depression, and paranoid tendency and should inquire about social and sexual patterns of withdrawal and passive dependency (Heller et al. 1974). Within the limits imposed by their physical condition, patients should be vigorously encouraged to participate as fully as possible in social activity. This will tend to improve the feelings of low self-esteem and helplessness associated with depression and passive dependence. Patients highly prone to post-operative disturbance can be identified preoperatively and might be managed by a number of prophylactic and psychotherapeutic techniques. Psychologically poorly adjusted patients are in the high risk group.

Sexual counseling is a vital part of the overall counseling and rehabilitation of the patient. A good sexual history will provide the framework and necessary data for proper counseling. Consideration of the patient's and the partner's concerns, fears, desires, and preferences is very important for effective counseling by the health professional. Reports of increased sexual satisfaction were positively correlated with the level of marital happiness (Jenkins et al. 1983). Furthermore, the emotional relationship becomes closer among those who resume sexual activity after surgery (Papadopoulos et al. 1986).

Apparently coronary bypass surgery does not abolish the misgivings about sexuality that frequently accompany symptoms of coronary artery disease, despite their elimination. Having received little or no counseling from staff, patients seem to set their own patterns for sexual behavior, which may represent a considerable deviation from premorbid activity (Thurer 1981). Perhaps those patients who do not resume pre-illness sexual behavior may benefit from sexual counseling. It was stated that such counseling of the patient and sometimes the partner, including specific recommendations, explanations, and reassurance, may help alleviate unnecessary anxiety and help restore the patient to active sexual life. In our study (Papadopoulos et al. 1986) however, of those who received sexual instructions, 82 percent stated that they did not fear resuming sexual activity and of those who did not receive any instructions, an equal percentage made a similar statement. Probably in many situations the counseling is not complete and comprehensive enough to alleviate all the anxiety and concerns of the patient.

We found that many of the previously sexually active patients who had CABG preferred to receive instructions together with their spouses. Wives often do not receive formal guidelines at the time of discharge of the patient from the hospital. Follow-up counseling in heart clubs or with individual couples is important because at times the patient and the partner are not ready for such information during the hospitalization. Occasionally the recollection of initial instructions is poor or the need to address new concerns and fears may develop. Providing written instructions before discharge from the hospital is often useful for better comprehension and recollection.

The counselor should be well acquainted with the patient's medical status and know the patient's physical limitations and psychological hindrances and his or her sexual fears and misconceptions. It is important that a permissive, relaxed atmosphere be maintained and that the physician demonstrates interest in and understanding of sexuality (Thurer and Thurer 1982). A positive attitude should be projected and it should be pointed out that sexual problems may often be overcome. Hope may engender success. In the study of women with CABG (Althof, Coffman and Levine 1984) it was stated that sexual counseling should not be indiscriminately offered to all women undergoing surgery. Many individuals have neither the relationship bond nor the ability to find sex pleasurable. It is unreasonable to expect an improvement in sexual functions in people with long-standing problematic relationships. Women with good pre-illness sexual functioning should be assured that the surgery will not permanently affect their sexuality.

Many bypass patients still view themselves as "heart patients" and as such they feel fragile, vulnerable, and as if they are living on borrowed time. Some are very reluctant to relinquish the sick role and unexpectedly these issues mitigate against a satisfying sex life. Furthermore, bypass patients may have been cardiac invalids for so long that they are out of practice. After protracted periods of non-indulgence in sex, they may have suppressed any interest and may not be able to resurrect it. For some individuals premorbid sexual problems may provide a good excuse for abstinence, an excuse unlikely to be forsaken with improvement in symptoms (Thurer and Thurer 1982).

Patients should be told that physical, sexual, and social recovery in some cases takes a matter of months, not weeks. Knowing in advance about the increased dependency and frustration may alleviate these burdens for the patient and the partner.

Effects of medications (such as beta-blockers) at times started after bypass surgery should be kept in mind because of their negative impact on sexuality. Often patients after cardiac surgery, especially for valve replacement, take anticoagulants and their effects — the appearance of bruises or hematomas after active sexual activity — should be considered and the patient reassured.

As the patients see their daily progress in their capacity for increasingly greater physical exertion, they lose some or all of their anxiety about the sexual act as a physical stress. The patients are usually encouraged to begin a gradual walking program and they progressively increase the speed and the distance (Weisberger 1985).

A treadmill exercise test and, if necessary, a 24-hour Holter recording, including the period of sexual activity, will provide further objective evaluation and reassurance for the patient. Participation in an exercise program based on the results of the treadmill exercise test will improve the physical tolerance and the psychological outlook of the patient.

BIBLIOGRAPHY

Althof, S. E., Coffman, C. B., Levine, S. B. 1984. "The effects of coronary bypass surgery on female sexual, psychological and vocational adaptation." *J of Sex and Marital Therapy* 10:176–84.

American Heart Association. 1988. "Heart Facts." Dallas: AHA Office of Communications.

Chestnut, D. H., Zlatnik, F. J., Pitkin, R. M. et al. 1986. "Pregnancy in a patient with a history of myocardial infarction and coronary artery bypass grafting." *Am J Obstet Gynecol* 155:372–73.

Davidson, D. M. 1983. "Return to work after cardiac events: A review." *J Cardiac Rehab* 3:60–69.

Frank, K. A., Heller, S. S., Kornfeld, D. S. 1972. "A survey of adjustment to cardiac surgery." *Arch Intern Med* 130:735–38.

Garson, A., Nihill, M. R., McNamara, D. G. et al. 1979. "Status of the adult and adolescent after repair of tetralogy of Fallot." *Circulation* 59:1232–40.

Gundle, M. J., Reeves, B. R., Tate, S. et al. 1980. "Psychosocial outcome after coronary artery surgery." *Am J Psych* 137:1591–94.

Hackett, T. P., Weisman, A. D. 1960. "Psychiatric management of operative syndromes." *Psychosomatic Med* 22:267–82.

Harvison, A., Jones, B. M., McBride, M. et al. 1988. "Rehabilitation after heart transplantation: The Australian experience." *J Heart Transplant* 7:337–41.

Heller, S. S., Frank, K. A., Kornfeld, D. S. et al. 1974. "Psychological outcome following open-heart surgery." *Arch Intern Med* 134:908–14.

Jenkins, C. D., Stanton, B. A., Savageau, J. A. et al. 1983. "Coronary artery bypass surgery: Physical, psychological, social and economic outcomes six months later." *JAMA* 250:782–88.

Johnston, B. L., Cantwell, J. D., Watt, E. W. et al. 1978. "Sexual activity in exercising patients after myocardial infarction and revascularization." *Heart & Lung* 7:1026–31.

Jones, B. M., Chang, V. P., Esmore, D. et al. 1988. "Psychological adjustment after cardiac transplantation." *Med J of Australia* 149:118–22.

Kinchla, J., Weiss, T. 1985. "Psychologic and social outcomes following coronary artery bypass surgery." *J Cardiopulmonary Rehab* 5:274–83.

Kornfeld, D. S., Heller, S. S., Frank, K. A. et al. 1982. "Psychological and behavioral responses after coronary artery bypass surgery." *Circulation* 66 (Suppl. III):24–28.

Kossoy, L. R., Herbert, C. M., Wentz, A. C. 1988. "Management of heart transplant recipients: Guidelines for the obstetrician-gynecologist." *Am J Obstet Gynecol* 159:490–99.

Levy, M. J., Benyakar, M., Mibashan, S. et al. 1985. "Sexual relations and the perception of health and happiness among patients following coronary artery bypass grafting and myocardial infarction." In *Return to work after coronary artery bypass surgery,* edited by P. J. Walter. New York: Springer-Verlag.

Lough, M. E., Shinn, J. A. 1987. "Impact of symptom frequency and symptom distress on self-reported quality of life in heart transplant recipients." *Heart & Lung* 16:193–200.

Lutz, D. J., Noller, K. L., Spittell, J. A. et al. 1978. "Pregnancy and its complications following cardiac valve prostheses." *Am J Obstet Gynecol* 131:460–68.

Oberman, A., Wayne, J. B., Kouchoukos, N. T. et al. 1982. "Employment status after coronary artery bypass surgery." *Circulation* 65:115–19.

Papadopoulos, C. 1978. "A survey of sexual activity after myocardial infarction." *Cardiovasc Med* 3:821–26.

____, Beaumont, C., Shelley, S. I. et al. 1983. "Myocardial infarction and sexual activity of the female patient." *Arch Intern Med* 143:1528–30.

____, Shelley, S. I., Piccolo, M. et al. 1986. "Sexual activity after coronary bypass surgery." *CHEST* 90:681–65.

Peduzzi, P., Hultgren, H. N. 1979. "Effect of medical vs. surgical treatment on symptoms in stable angina pectoris. The Veterans Administration Cooperative Study of Surgery for Coronary Arterial Occlusive Disease." *Circulation* 60:888–900.

Penckofer, S. H., Holm, K. 1984. "Early appraisal of coronary revascularization on quality of life." *Nursing Research* 33:60–63.

Perloff, J. K. 1973. "Pediatric congenital cardiac becomes a postoperative adult." *Circulation* 17:606–19.

Raft, D., McKee, D. C., Popio, K. A. et al. 1985. "Life adaptation after percutaneous transluminal coronary angioplasty and coronary artery bypass grafting." *Am J Cardiol* 56:395–98.

Rahimtoola, S. H. 1982. "Coronary bypass surgery for chronic angina — 1981." *Circulation* 65:225–41.

Reece, E. A., Egan, J. F. X., Coustan, D. R. et al. 1986. "Coronary artery disease in diabetic pregnancies." *Am J. Obstet Gynecol* 154:150–51.

Ross, J. K., Diwell, A. E., Marsh, J. et al. 1978. "Wessex cardiac surgery followup survey: The quality of life after operation." *Thorax* 33:3–9.

Schroeder, J. S., Hunt, S. A. 1986. "Cardiac transplantation: Where are we?" *N Engl J Med* 315:961–63.

Sikorski, J. M. 1985. "Knowledge, concerns, and questions of wives of convalescent coronary artery bypass graft surgery patients." *J Cardiac Rehab* 5:74–85.

Smith, H. C., Hammes, L. N., Gupta, S. et al. 1982. "Employment status after coronary bypass surgery." *Circulation* 65 (Suppl. II):120–25.

Smith, H. C. 1985. "Quality of life after coronary artery bypass surgery." *Quality of Life and Cardiovascular Care* 1:215–28.

Thurer, S. 1981. "Sexual adjustment following coronary bypass surgery." *Rehab Counseling Bulletin* 24:319–22.

____, Thurer, R. L. 1982. "Sex after coronary bypass surgery." *Med Asp of Hum Sex* 16:68F–68K.

Wiesberger, C. L. 1985. "Sexual counseling for the patient following coronary artery surgery." *Med Asp Hum Sex* 19:137–41.

Westaby, S., Sapsford, R. N., Bentall, H. H. 1979. "Return to work and quality of life after surgery for coronary artery disease." *British Med J* 2:1028–31.

Zyzanski, S. J., Stanton, B. A., Jenkins, C. D. et al. 1981. "Medical and psychosocial outcomes in survivors of major heart surgery." *Psychosom Res* 23:213–21.

4

Sexual Function, Aorto-iliac Occlusive Disease and Surgery

Sexual dysfunction is one of the protean manifestations of aorto-iliac occlusive disease. Impotence is often an early manifestation of arteriosclerotic occlusion of the common iliac and internal iliac vessels. Sexual problems are common among individuals undergoing vascular reconstructive surgery for aorto-iliac occlusive disease. At other times the dysfunction is the post-operative result of aorto-iliac surgery.

Among men referred to a vascular service for evaluation of peripheral arterial disease, 40 to 50 percent complained of erectile dysfunction (Wagner and Green 1981). The reported incidence of impotence in aorto-iliac occlusive disease varies from 40 to 80 percent (Goldstein 1984). The relationship between arteriosclerosis and erectile failure has been known since Leriche and Morel (1948) described patients with arterial thrombosis and occlusion of the aortic bifurcation associated with erectile failure.

For many years the medical literature stated that erectile impotence was caused by psychogenic factors in 90 percent of patients, but more recently refined diagnostic techniques have shown that up to 50 percent of patients may have organic impotence (Carson 1981). Many men previously labeled psychogenically impotent have been shown to have vascular compromise to their pelvic organs (Malloy and Wein 1983). In a study using phalloarteriography it was estimated that 25 percent of impotent men have erectile dysfunction due to arterial disease (Ginestie and Romieu 1978).

ANATOMY AND PHYSIOLOGY

A full appreciation of the mechanism underlying sexual dysfunction from aorto-iliac occlusive disease and of the role surgery plays in correcting the problem requires an understanding of the anatomy and physiology of erection (Warwick and Williams 1973; Masters and Johnson 1966; Weiss 1978; Papadopoulos 1980; DeGroat and Booth 1980; Malloy and Wein 1983).

Penile erection is a reflex phenomenon initiated by psychic or physical stimulation. Afferent impulses from sensory branches of thedorsal nerve of the penis reach the sacral cord via the pudendal nerve. Reflex parasympathetic impulses pass from the sacral cord to the penis via the nervi erigentes, resulting in engorgement of the penile vessels and venous sinuses leading to erection.

Sympathetic fibers may also be involved in this process. As sexual stimulation intensifies, reflex impulses in the lumbar cord are triggered and sexual climax is initiated by sympathetic impulses from the thoracolumbar autonomic outflow (T12-L3), which lead to emission of semen into the posterior part of the urethra. This is the trigger that excites afferent impulses via the pudendal nerve to the sacral cord (S2, S3 and S4) and returns as a reflex arch along the same nerve to contract the pelvic and perineal musculature. Sympathetic outflow simultaneously inhibits the muscle wall of the bladder and tightens the internal urethral sphincter, preventing retrograde ejaculation.

Erection is a vascular phenomenon. The arterial blood supply is derived from the aorta, which divides into the common iliac arteries. These divide into the external and internal (hypogastric) vessels. The latter become the internal pudendal arteries after sending a large branch vessel to the gluteal muscles. The pudendal artery becomes the penile artery, which divides into the urethral artery, the deep penile artery and the dorsal artery. The paired deep penile arteries provide the arterial supply to the main erectile tissue, the corpora cavernosa. The erectile tissues consist of irregular sponge-like systems of vascular spaces interspersed between the arteries and veins. The distention of the penis with blood during erection is brought about by the opening of anastomoses between the arterioles and the vascular spaces in the erectile tissues where valve-like structures containing smooth muscle are located. These structures are under the control of the autonomic nervous system (fibers from the sacral and lumbar erection centers) and relax when impulses for erection are transmitted, thereby allowing a greatly increased volume of blood to flow into the vascular spaces of the erectile tissues. The rate of arterial inflow is temporarily greater than the rate of venous outflow, thus causing the characteristic increase in penile volume. Similar valve-like structures on the venous side may contract and diminish venous outflow. A steady state is eventually reached. The mechanism for subsidence of penile erection is not clearly understood. It is not known whether this is merely due to diminution of the cholinergic (vasodilator) impulses that open the valve-like structures or whether an active vasoconstrictor impulse is also involved. It is obvious that obstruction or disease at any level from the aorta to the small penile artery can cause sexual dysfunction and impotence.

The venous drainage from the penis is divided into a superficial system that drains into the superficial dorsal vein. The deep veins that form the drainage system for the erectile tissue drain into the deep vein of the penis and subsequently into the Santorini's plexus of veins. The existence of valvules in the deep dorsal vein and in the pelvic venous system has been demonstrated (Fitzpatrick 1974). If the valvules become incompetent there is a "venous leak." The deep dorsal vein also has sphincters under neurologic control that allow the regulation of blood outflow from the corpora cavernosa (Delcour et al. 1984).

It appears that the resting blood flow through the penile artery is low, 10 ml/minute, which is approximately 1 percent of the total blood flow through the common iliac arteries. During sexual stimulation a sixfold increase of inflow has been shown to occur in the internal pudendal and penile arteries in the normal individual. If only a three- or fourfold increase of arterial blood flow can be achieved because of various degrees of atherosclerosis within the hypogastric-cavernous arterial bed, a partial erection will result. If the stenosis is proximal and involves the origin of both hypogastric arteries, patients may exhibit a "steal phenomenon." They may be able to develop an erection under resting conditions, but when they undergo coital movement restrictive pelvic blood inflow is redirected to the gluteal muscle bed away from the corporal bodies. These patients may lose their erections during coital activity. Patients with severe distal disease may be clinically distinguished by the total inability to develop an erection, even at rest.

VASCULOGENIC IMPOTENCE

Patient Evaluation

Diagnosis of vasculogenic impotence requires an organized and detailed evaluation which several authors have emphasized (Nath et al. 1981; Carson 1981; Malloy and Wein 1983; Goldstein et al. 1984). A detailed general medical and sexual history must be obtained. A complete physical examination and appropriate laboratory tests will be needed. Psychologic, neurologic, endocrine, and metabolic causes of impotence should be ruled out. A history of morning erections is important and may be an indication that erections are physiologically possible. Gradual episodic loss of erectile ability may indicate organic impotence. The quality, state, and duration of the erections should be specifically determined.

When impotence is due to atherosclerotic occlusive disease there will often be early symptoms suggesting this diagnostic possibility. The physician should ascertain if the patient is suffering from intermittent claudication (Machleder 1978). The symptom of an aching muscular cramp in the hip, thigh or buttocks that is brought on by walking and relieved by several moments of rest is frequently observed in patients with aortic-iliac occlusive disease. Careful questioning to elicit the "pelvic steal syndrome" should be included in the history taking. History of diabetes and the use of alcohol and drugs must be carefully recorded.

A complete physical examination is important, including the genitalia. Indurated Peyronie's plaques may be palpated on the dorsal surface of the penis. Testicular failure may be manifested by small atrophic testes and a small involuted prostate. A neurologic and vascular examination should be included. Lower extremity pulses, especially femoral and pedal pulses, should be checked. If vascular disease is suspected, penile blood pressure, using a digital blood pressure cuff and Doppler stethoscope, should be used to gauge penile blood supply. The penile systolic pressure is compared to the brachial systolic pressure to obtain the penile-brachial index (PBI). A PBI of less than .6 is diagnostic of vasculogenic impotence, while a PBI of .6 to .75 is compatible with, but not diagnostic of, this condition. "Pelvic steal syndrome" is tested by obtaining the PBI at rest and after exercising the legs for three minutes or until claudication symptoms develop. A drop in the PBI may be noticed.

In certain cases, internal pudendal arteriograms are of great help in diagnosis. In younger individuals, the vascular occlusions noted may be related to trauma with subsequent development of intimal hyperplasia instead of atherosclerosis. Erectile insufficiency seen in patients with pelvic fractures after motor vehicle accidents may be related to traumatic vascular disease.

Cavernosography, a radiologic contrast infusion procedure that allows the study of corpora cavernosa and the venous drainage, and monitoring of intracavernous pressure have recently been described. They explain venous conditions causing erectile dysfunction in patients with normal arterial anatomy (Delcour et al. 1984).

Laboratory evaluation should include complete blood count, blood chemistry profile, serum testosterone, luteinizing hormone, follicle stimulating hormone, prolactin, thyroid studies, and glucose tolerance tests. At times special neurologic evaluation, including electromyographic studies of the perineum, are indicated.

Specific procedures to document erectile ability may be carried out. These include nocturnal penile tumescence (NPT) monitoring. Through the use of transducers at the base and tip of the penis a patient can be monitored throughout the night and nocturnal erections observed in association with rapid eye movement (REM) sleep. Patients with organic impotence have absent or markedly decreased nocturnal erectile frequency.

Treatment

Treatment of vasculogenic impotence by medical means is virtually nonexistent. A single case of atherosclerotic impotence with good response to nitrates has been reported (Mudd 1977). However, successful coitus has recently been described in cases of vasculogenic impotence after auto-injection of the corpus cavernosum with papaverine hydrochloride and phentolamine mesylate (Zorgniotti and Lefleur 1985; Sidi et al. 1985).

Surgery to correct vascular insufficiency has been successful when the lesions have been proximally located in the great vessels, such as the aorta and iliac vessels (Malloy and Wein 1983). When the pathology is distal, in the pudendal and penile arteries, the surgical results have been discouraging. Various penile revascularization techniques have been attempted, including inferior epigastric-dorsal artery bypass and femoro-pudendal bypass. Epigastric-corporal shunts and femoro-corporal shunts have also been used. Initial results are successful, but tend to fail within several months. In a recent report (Hawatmeh et al. 1981) five patients underwent femoro-cavernosal bypass with an autogenous saphenous vein graft. Initial results were excellent, but late failures occurred and at 28 months all shunts were occluded. Microscopic examination of the cavernous tissue revealed fibrous thickening of the septa and loss of cavernous spaces. These findings suggested that late failure in direct revascularization may be associated with fibrotic changes that occur under high pressure inflow to the corpora cavernosa.

Selective ligation of the deep dorsal vein in cases of impotence attributed to "venous leak" from incompetence of the vein valvules provided a cure rate of 75 percent (Delcour et al. 1984). Anastomosis of the femoral artery to the deep penile vein by a saphenous vein graft, together with ligation of the superficial veins at the base of the penis, has also been used for impotence due to venous leakage (Balko et al. 1986).

Balloon angioplasty of internal iliac and/or internal pudendal artery obstructions for vasculogenic impotence is adequate and expeditious (Angelini and Fighali 1987).

Surgical insertion of penile prostheses (either inflatable or of the semirigid rod type) currently offers more reliable treatment for vasculogenic impotence. Several articles (Furlow 1978; Scott et al. 1979; Malloy, Wein and Carpiniello 1982) have reported on series of patients in whom excellent results were obtained utilizing the inflatable penile prosthesis.

POST-OPERATIVE SEXUAL DYSFUNCTION

Sexual dysfunction secondary to surgical procedures for correction of atherosclerotic aorto-iliac disease, whether aneurysm or obstruction, often occurs. Lumbar sympathectomy, involving bilateral removal of the first and second lumbar ganglia in men, is usually followed by a loss of ejaculation (Lord 1973). Unilateral removal of L1 through L4 should have no effect. The patient should be informed of the probable change in sexual function, which usually follows bilateral lumbar sympathectomy. According to the same author (Lord 1973) bilateral lumbar sympathectomy in women has had no obvious effect on sexual function.

Sexual disturbances following operation on the aorta and the common iliac arteries is a significant problem. In many patients with aorto-iliac occlusive disease, sexual dysfunction may be present preoperatively, but one-quarter to one-half of patients may experience new problems with erection and ejaculation in the post-operative period (May, DeWeese and Rob 1969; Hallbook and Holmquist 1970; Weinstein and Machleder 1974; Smead and Vaccaro 1983). This is believed to be related to failure to restore or maintain internal iliac flow, precipitation of atheroemboli into the pelvic circulation, or interruption of the neural plexi at the level of the inferior mesenteric artery, aortic bifurcation, and left common iliac artery (DePalma 1982). In one series (May, DeWeese and Rob 1969) 44 male patients who underwent surgery for occlusive disease of the distal aorta or iliac arteries and 26 who had surgery for aneurysm were interviewed in person concerning changes in sexual function after surgery. Eight percent of patients with aneurysms and 70 percent of patients with aorto-iliac obstruction had some preoperative impairment of erection. After operation, impairment of erection developed in 21 percent of sexually normal patients having aneurysmectomy and in 34 percent of normal patients having revascularization for occlusive disease. Sixty-three percent of patients having aneurysmectomy and 49 percent of those having surgery for aorto-iliac obstruction developed post-operative abnormalities of ejaculation. In sexually normal patients, when the lower end of the reconstruction was completed above the external iliac arteries, 20 percent developed impaired erection. When the reconstruction was completed below the origins of the external iliac arteries, there was impairment in 44 percent. Extensive aorto-iliac dissection, such as for thromboendarterectomy or aneurysm resection resulted in post-operative abnormalities of ejaculation in 50 to 75 percent of patients, whereas bypass graft reconstruction for occlusive disease caused abnormal ejaculation in 26 percent of patients.

In another series (Hallbook and Holmquist 1970) 36 consecutive male patients who had been subjected to more or less extensive dissection of the lower part of the abdominal aorta and iliac vessels were questioned concerning sexual dysfunction after the operation. Of the 31 who responded, 14 reported disturbances. Four had become impotent, while ten were still potent but reported absence of ejaculation. In most of these patients the dissection of the aortic bifurcation had been extensive. It was felt that interference with the hypogastric sympathetic nerves and the hypogastric plexus during the operation will result in failure of closure of the internal urethral sphincter and consequent disturbance of the mechanism of ejaculation.

In a small series of 20 patients who had aorto-iliac surgery (Weinstein and Machleder 1974) 80 percent complained post-operatively of retrograde ejaculation and 10 percent of impotence. Dissection of the sympathetic fibers around the abdominal aorta as high as the level of the inferior mesenteric artery and as low as the bifurcation of the aorta appears to result in either loss of potency or ejaculation. All of the patients in this study who complained of loss of ejaculation underwent abdominal aortic aneurysmectomy.

The inferior mesenteric and the superior and inferior hypogastric plexuses lie on the anterior surface of the aorta, just above the iliac bifurcation and extend downward over the iliac arteries as they descend into the pelvis. These parasympathetic and sympathetic nerves are sacrificed in the resection of an abdominal aortic aneurysm. If the aneurysm ends above the bifurcation, the inferior hypogastric plexus and a portion of the superior hypogastric plexus can be spared. Resection of an abdominal aneurysm usually destroys branches of S2, S3 and S4, as well as L2 and L3. This impairs much of the parasympathetic and sympathetic nerve supply; thus, a major portion of the efferent nerve supply controlling erection is impaired (Edwards 1977). In addition to changes in erection, changes also occur in ejaculation. Emission of semen into the posterior urethra is the trigger impulse that excites afferent impulses via the pudendal nerve to S2, S3 and S4 and returns as a reflex arch along the same nerve to contract the pelvic and perineal musculature. Complete failure of emission and ejaculation or retrograde ejaculation frequently occur after resection of an abdominal aneurysm. The sensation of ejaculation is retained in retrograde ejaculation but is lost with failure of emission.

Extreme caution in the dissection of the aortic bifurcation is necessary. Gentleness in the handling of tissue and minimization of dissection are important to avoid possible pelvic atheroembolization and disruption of important neural plexi. The operation should be designed to preserve flow into the internal iliac arteries and at no time should these vessels be sacrificed unnecessarily. For aneurysmal disease, the inclusion grafting technique is preferred and the longitudinal opening in the aorta should be made as far to the right of the orifice of the inferior mesenteric artery as possible to avoid the neural elements (Smead and Vaccaro 1983). In the presence of iliac aneurysm it has been suggested that the left limb of the bifurcated graft be passed through the undisturbed sac of the left common iliac aneurysm and carried down to its appropriate distal position, thus preserving neural continuity (Weinstein and Machleder 1974). For occlusive disease an end to side rather than an end to end proximal aortic anastomosis may at times be performed to maintain the pelvic circulation through the patient's own aorta. Careful retroperitoneal tunneling of the distal limbs of the graft should not disturb neural continuity.

COUNSELING PRIOR TO SURGERY

Prior to surgery the physician should explain to the patient and his partner what sexual changes might occur. The sexual function of the patient should be preoperatively evaluated and the possibility of post-operative impotence or retrograde ejaculation should be discussed. Understanding the phenomenon of retrograde ejaculation and of possible erectile changes may prevent fears and anxieties from appearing after surgery. If impotence develops, the partners may consider alternate expressions of sexual feelings or an implantable penile prosthesis.

BIBLIOGRAPHY

Angelini, P., Fighali, S. 1987. "Early experience with balloon angioplasty of internal iliac arteries for vasculogenic impotence." *Cathet Cardiovasc Diagn* 13:107–10.

Balko, A., Malhotra, C., Wincze, J. et al. 1986. "Deep-penile-vein arterialization for arterial and venous impotence." *Arch Surg* 121: 774–77.

Carson, C. C. 1981. "Evaluation of impotence." *Med Asp of Hum Sex* 15:137–38.

DeGroat, W. C., Booth, A. M. 1980. "Physiology of male sexual function." *Ann of Int Med* 92:329–31.

Delcour, C., Wespes, E., Schulman, C. C. et al. 1984. "Investigation of the venous system in impotence of vascular origin." *Urol Radiol* 6:190–93.

DePalma, R. G. 1982. "Impotence in vascular disease: Relationship to vascular surgery." *Br J Surg* (Suppl.) S14.

Edwards, W. H. 1977. "Abdominal aortic aneurysmectomy and impaired sexual function." *Med Asp of Hum Sex* 11:67–68.

Fitzpatrick, T. J. 1974. "Venography of the deep dorsal venous and valvular systems." *J Urol* 111:518–20.

Furlow, W. L. 1978, "Surgical management of impotence using the inflatable penile prosthesis: Experience with 103 patients." *Br J Urol* 50:114–17.

Ginestie, J. F., Romieu, A. 1978. *Radiologic exploration of impotence*. The Hague, Netherlands: Martinos Nighoff.

Goldstein, I. 1984. "Vasculogenic impotence." *Med Asp of Hum Sex* 18:134–44.

Hallbook, T., Holmquist, B. 1970. "Sexual disturbances following dissection of the aorta and the common iliac arteries." *J Cardiovasc Surg* 4:255–60.

Hawatmeh, I. S., Houttuin, E., Gregory, J. G. et al. 1981. "The diagnosis and surgical management of vasculogenic impotence." *Urol* 127:910–14.

Leriche, R., Morel, A. 1948. "The syndrome of thrombotic obliteration at the aortic bifurcation." *Ann Surg* 127:193–206.

Lord, J. W. 1973. "Peripheral vascular disorders and sexual function." *Med Asp of Hum Sex* 7:34–43.

Machleder, H. I. 1978. "Sexual dysfunction in aorto-iliac occlusive disease." *Med Asp of Hum Sex* 12:125–26.

Malloy, T. R., Wein, A. J. 1983. "Penile flaccidity due to vascular insufficiency." *Med Asp of Hum Sex* 17:211–20.

____, Wein, A. J., Carpiniello, V. L. 1982. "Improved mechanical survival with revised model inflatable penile prosthesis utilizing rear tip extenders." *J Urol* 128:489–91.

Masters, W. H., Johnson, V. E. 1966. *Human sexual response.* pp. 177–88. Boston: Little, Brown.

May, A. G., DeWeese, J. A., Rob, C. G. 1969. "Changes in sexual function following operation on the abdominal aorta." *Surgery* 65:41–47.

Mudd, J. W. 1977. "Impotence responsive to glyceryl trinitrate." *Am J Psych* 134:922–25.

Nath, R. L., Menzoian, J. O., Kaplan, K. H. et al. 1981. "The multidisciplinary approach to vasculogenic impotence." *Surgery* 89:124–33.

Papadopoulos, C. 1980. "Cardiovascular drugs and sexuality: A cardiologist's review." *Arch Intern Med* 140:1341–45.

Scott, F. B., Byrd, G. J., Karacan, I. et al. 1979. "Erectile impotence treated with an implantable, inflatable prosthesis." *JAMA* 241:2609–12.

Sidi, A. A., Cameron, J. S., Duffy, L. M. et al. 1985. "Intravenous drug-induced erections in the management of male erectile dysfunction: Experience with 100 patients." *J Urol* 135:704–06.

Smead, W. L., Vaccaro, P. S. 1983. "Infrarenal aortic aneurysmectomy." *Surg Clin of North Amer* 63:1269–92.

Wagner, G., Green, R. 1981. *Impotence.* p. 63. New York: Plenum Press.

Warwick, R., Williams, P. L. 1973. *Gray's Anatomy.* 35th ed. Philadelphia: W. B. Saunders.

Weinstein, M. H., Machleder, H. I. 1974. "Sexual function after aorto-iliac surgery." *Ann Surg* 181:787–90.

Weiss, H. D. 1978. "The physiology of human penile erection." In *Sexual consequences of disability,* edited by Alex Comfort, pp. 11–24. Philadelphia: G. F. Stickley.

Zorgniotti, A. W., Lefleur, R. S. 1985. "Auto-injection of the corpus carvernosum with a vasoactive drug combination for vasculogenic impotence." *J Urol* 133:39–41.

5
Sex and the Hypertensive Patient

More than 60 million persons in the United States have either been found to have elevated blood pressure (140/90 mm Hg or greater) or have been told by a physician that they have hypertension (Joint National Committee on Detection 1984). Prevalence rates increase with age in the U.S. population and the rate for black Americans far exceeds the rate for whites (Rowland and Robert 1982). The risk related to hypertension increases continuously as systolic and diastolic blood pressure rise (Kannel 1976). Data from the Framingham study (Kannel and Dawber 1974) showed that hypertension is the greatest contributor to morbidity and mortality from cardiovascular disease, that labile blood pressure leads to fixed hypertension, and casual blood pressure elevation is strongly related to cardiovascular morbidity and mortality.

Stroke, myocardial infarction, congestive heart failure, and renal failure are known complications of hypertension. Therefore the sexuality of the hypertensive patient may be affected, not only by the disease itself and its treatment, but also by its complications.

PHYSIOLOGIC AND PATHOLOGIC ASPECTS

Physiologic and pathologic problems may arise from the expenditure of sexual energy in the presence of moderate or significant hypertension since exertional and emotional stress further elevate blood pressure. Only a few data on the response of blood pressure to sexual activity are available for normotensives and even less for hypertensive patients. The results of these studies, which usually involve a very small number of people, are not consistent and show variation from moderate to marked elevations of systolic and diastolic pressure.

That sexual arousal produced consistent elevations of heart rate and blood pressure in young men was shown many years ago (Scott 1930). An exhaustive study of the anatomy and physiology of human sexual response, using adult men and women who were willing to serve as subjects in the laboratory, revealed marked increases in heart rate and arterial blood pressure during sexual intercourse (Masters and Johnson 1966). The investigators observed in the male increases in systolic pressure of 40 to 100 mm Hg and in diastolic pressure of 20 to 50 mm Hg, and in the female increases of 30 to 80 mm Hg and 20 to 40 mm Hg, respectively.

It was felt that these results may have been affected by the environment to which these subjects were exposed.

In a report of a study carried out in the habitual environment of their own bedroom with one married couple with ten years of mutual coital experience, with orgasm achieved by both partners, the systolic pressure rose by 100 mm to a peak of 200 mm Hg in the female and by 65 to a peak of 175 mm Hg in the male. Both the peak figures were obtained after orgasm (Fox and Fox 1969).

Ten males (24 to 40 years of age) were studied during four episodes of sexual intercourse with their wives in their homes. The heart rate and blood pressure responses were recorded with a portable ECG tape recorder and an automatic ultrasonic BP recorder (Nemec, Mansfield and Kennedy 1964). They studied each couple during two sessions with the male on top and two sessions with the male on the bottom. There were essentially no differences in heart rate, systolic blood pressure, or diastolic blood pressure at various phases of intercourse in the two positions. An average blood pressure of 162/79 mm Hg at orgasm was reported.

In a study of direct arterial blood pressure, heart rate, and the electrocardiogram of 72 subjects over a 24-hour period, there were 7 normotensives (6 males and 1 female) who had sexual intercourse in their home environment during the 24-hour period of the study (Littler, Honour and Sleight 1974). The system used included an intra-arterial teflon catheter, a transducer, a perfusion pump, and a tape recording system. The duration of intercourse ranged from 8 to 20 minutes and orgasm was achieved by all 6 males, but not by the female. Significant changes in arterial systolic and diastolic pressure and heart rate were noted compared with values at the onset of coitus. Systolic pressure rose by 20 to 107 percent (25 to 120 mm Hg), diastolic pressure by 31 to 60 percent (25 to 48 mm Hg), and heart rate increased by 25 to 120 percent (+20 to 87 beats/minute). Peak arterial pressure and heart rate occurred at the time of orgasm, after which arterial pressure and, to a lesser extent, heart rate quickly fell to below the precoital level within 20 to 120 seconds.

In an investigation of patients with hypertension, a large number of ambulatory recordings of intra-arterial pressures were performed, a cannula was inserted percutaneously in the brachial artery of the subject and connected to a transducer/perfusion device. Signals from this and from chest electrocardiographic electrodes were recorded on two channels of cassette taping using a miniature recording (Mann et al. 1982). Enough wire was provided to allow the subject to position the recorder either behind him or at his side when lying flat. Eighteen episodes of coitus were recorded in 11 subjects. The mean age of the subjects was 42 (range 29 to 56 years). The group included three women. The recordings showed that both heart rate and blood pressure fluctuated widely during sexual activity, occasionally reaching very high levels. Although patterns varied greatly, the highest peaks of heart rate and blood pressure (presumably associated with orgasm) were generally simultaneous and were followed by a rapid fall to precoital levels. The peak blood pressures were very high, the mean being 237/133 mm Hg (range 184–300/92–175 mm Hg) for men and 216/127 mm Hg (range 190–260/110–155 mm Hg) for women. These levels were sustained in each case for only a few seconds. Peak heart rates were 130/minute and 96/minute for men and women respectively. From this study it was apparent that those subjects starting with higher baseline levels reached corresponding higher peak pressures during coitus.

The response to exercise is complex, involving a number of variables, including heart rate, stroke volume, sympathetic activity, excitement, apprehension, straining, and position. The increased sympathetic activity during sexual emotion and exercise causes increased catecholamine release, which results in both increased cardiac rate and increased ventricular contractility. One of the hallmarks of hypertensive patients is the increased vascular reactivity to catecholamines (Howard 1973). Hypertension increases left ventricular work and eventually causes left ventricular hypertrophy, impaired left ventricular function, and reduced cardiac output.

One should consider that with exertion and sexual activity the potential for the uncontrolled hypertensive to develop angina, arrhythmias, or pulmonary edema exists. The severe hypertensive's cerebrovascular system is especially vulnerable. This system has a remarkable capacity for self-regulation in dealing with both high and low systemic arterial pressures, but when they exceed 200 mm Hg the autoregulatory protection is overcome. Elevation of systemic and cerebral arterial blood pressure up to 180 or 200 mm Hg will cause cerebral arterioles to constrict, thus protecting the distal arterioles and capillaries, but beyond this level capillary pressures will rise, increasing the perfusion pressure. Intense vasospasm may then occur and cause distal microinfarction, rupture with hemorrhage or transudation with cerebral edema (Howard 1973). Effort leading to Valsalva maneuver response during coitus may lead to increased capillary perfusion pressures in the brain.

Headache associated with sexual activity and orgasm may be severe, frightening, and occasionally tragic (Paulson 1982), though the causes are variable. It may represent a migraine variant or neck muscle tightness or be related to sexual excitement in someone exposed to heat, vasodilatory drugs, or alcohol. If the patient is hypertensive, pheochromocytoma or other treatable causes of hypertension must be considered. In rare cases subarachnoid hemorrhage may be the cause.

EMOTIONAL AND PSYCHOLOGICAL ASPECTS

Emotional and psychological factors may further contribute to the effect of sexual activity on blood pressure. The physiologic response to emotional stress varies in different individuals and whether one is a "hot reactor" or "cold reactor" will have a significantly different response on the blood pressure (Buell 1984). The "hot reactor," under mental stress, has a direct dramatic physiologic reaction with marked elevation of blood pressure, while a "cold reactor" has normal cardiovascular responses. Because of the variability of external stimuli and physiologic reaction in the field, the diagnosis of the hot reactor is best established in the laboratory through a set of standardized tasks, performed in a controlled environment. The subject's hemodynamic responses are monitored through an oscillometric blood pressure unit and an impedance cardiographic system, including electrocardiography. Technicians in another room observe the patient on closed-circuit television and monitor his physiologic responses, while a computer calculates hemodynamic values. A video game, a serial subtraction arithmetic test, and a cold pressure test (dipping a hand in ice water) are used.

Anxiety and frustration from sexual difficulties may further exacerbate the elevated blood pressure of hypertensives during sexual activity. Such life changes as the death of a spouse, divorce, marital separation, and other sexual-emotional changes have a powerful effect on psychophysiologic reactions (Petrich and Holmes 1977).

RISKS

The incidence of cerebrovascular accidents according to the levels of systolic blood pressure is remarkable. However, there is no convincing evidence that hypertensive patients are particularly susceptible to acute cardiovascular catastrophes during sexual intercourse. Gifford (1973) stated that in his personal experience in treating hundreds of hypertensive patients over 20 years, no instance of cardiac or cerebral accident occurred during sexual activity. The exact incidence, though it appears to be small, may not be known since the circumstances under which such accidents occur are probably rarely reported.

In a series of 5,559 cases of sudden death, 34 or 0.6 percent occurred during intercourse. Though most of the cases among males were from cardiac causes, four of the six female cases were due to cerebral hemorrhage (Ueno 1963). It was not stated, however, how many of these were hypertensive. In a report of obscure causes of death during sexual activity (Beyer and Enos 1977), it was noted that the incidence of ruptured berry aneurysm of the cerebral arteries, with subarachnoid hemorrhage during or after sexual intercourse, is relatively low. In the authors' medical examiners files there was one case of intracerebral hemorrhage that occurred in a middle-aged white female following an extramarital affair. A case of coincident rupture of berry aneurysm and aortic dissection during sexual intercourse was recently reported (Lovas and Silver 1984). While engaged in sexual intercourse, a 34-year-old man had a severe headache, lapsed into a coma, and became apneic. He had a 16-year history of systemic hypertension treated with diuretics, but no recent blood pressure measurements were available.

SEXUAL DYSFUNCTIONS

In a comparative study of the complaints recorded on a questionnaire by normotensive subjects, untreated hypertensives, and hypertensive patients on long-term treatment (Bulpitt, Dollery and Carne 1976), information on sexual dysfunction was included. Impotence was described in 17.1 percent of untreated hypertensive men (average age 51 years) compared with only 6.9 percent of normotensive men (average age 53 years). There was 7.3 percent incidence of ejaculation failure among the untreated hypertensives in comparison to no incidence of such a complaint among the normal subjects. In another report 20 percent of untreated hypertensives presented impotence and 10 percent "failed ejaculation" with the incidence being 10 percent and 6 percent, respectively, among normals (Moss and Procci 1982). Explanation of these differences could only be speculative. Organic causes may play a role. Furthermore, learning that one suffers from hypertension may cause fear and anxiety, which may lead to sexual dysfunction, even before medications are started. Patients with hypertension may also present with congestive heart failure, dyspnea, or angina, which may limit the sexual activities because of the symptoms and the fear generated.

Hypertensive patients with chronic renal failure are azotemic and ill and this leads to severe deterioration in the patient's sexual relationship due to loss of desire, partial, or total impotence in the male or anorgasmia in the female. An extensive study of patients who had reached the level of hemodialysis (Levy 1973) revealed substantial deterioration in sexual function in comparing the status of the patient at the time of the interview with that prior to the development of uremia. While emotional factors (Levy 1973) may play a role, uremic neuropathy (Guevara 1969), hormonal imbalances (Lim, Auletta and Kathpalia 1978), and drugs also play a role.

EFFECTS OF ANTIHYPERTENSIVE DRUGS

Antihypertensive medications play a major role in sexual dysfunction of the hypertensive patient. In a recent study of such therapy among 861 patients, sexual dysfunction was reported by 101 or 12.6 percent of the patients (Hogan, Wallin and Baer 1980). These patients were on various medications. A positive history for sexual dysfunction was found in 9 percent of patients receiving a diuretic (hydrochlorothiazide) alone, 13 percent of those receiving methyldopa, 15 percent receiving clonidine and 23 percent treated with propranolol and hydralazine in combination. The incidence of dysfunction in 177 control patients was 4 percent.

Antihypertensive medications may act by decreasing water and electrolyte levels, interfering with efferent sympathetic activity, causing vasodilatation, or modifying the renin-angiotensin system. These pharmacologic agents may affect the libido and the erectile and orgasmic phases of sexuality. In general, the effects of drugs on male sexuality are far better described and understood than is their influence on the responses of females, particularly because the male response is more visible and quantifiable.

Practically all groups of antihypertensive medications may have sexual side effects. They may affect the sexuality of the patient by acting on the central or peripheral nervous system, the vascular system, or through hormonal changes (Papadopoulos 1980; see also Chapter 7).

Diuretics.

Though in the past the effect of diuretics was anecdotal, there is now more evidence accumulating that they may cause loss of libido, impotence, and inhibition of vaginal lubrication. Spironolactone has more significant effects, causing decrease of libido, impotence, irregular menses, amenorrhea, post-menopausal bleeding, and hirsutism. Gynecomastia is a fairly frequent complication and may be associated with mastodynia. Amiloride and triamterene may also cause impotence, in rare cases.

Adrenergic antagonists.

Beta-blockers, such as propranolol, may cause reduced libido, impotence, and Peyronie's disease. Alpha-adrenergic blockers such as prasozin may cause a very small incidence of impotence. Centrally acting adrenergic inhibitors, such as clonidine, guanabenz, and methyldopa may lead to impotence, ejaculation difficulties, loss of libido or gynecomastia. Inability to achieve orgasm in women has also been reported with clonidine. Peripheral acting adrenergic inhibitors, such as guanadrel, guanethidine, and Rauwolfia alkaloids have been known to cause impotence, ejaculation difficulties, and loss of libido.

Vasodilators.

Hydralazine and minoxidil belong to this group and usually have no sexual side effects, although hydralazine in very high doses may cause loss of libido.

Recently new groups of medications are being used for hypertension and they too may present sexual side effects.

Alpha and beta adrenergic receptor blockers.

Labetalol has been reported to cause loss of libido, "dry ejaculation," and impotence in some cases.

Slow channel calcium-entry blocking agents.

Some cases have been reported to develop impotence or gynecomastia.

Angiotensin-converting enzyme (ACE) inhibitors.

Not much information is yet available as to their sexual effects. They are thought not to cause sexual dysfunction, though in rare cases impotence may occur.

REHABILITATION AND COUNSELING

A careful history and medical evaluation of the hypertensive patient is vital in trying to eliminate reasons for hypertension, such as the use of medications that may be causing the elevated blood pressure (oral contraceptives, steroidal and nonsteroidal anti-inflammatory agents, nasal decongestants, appetite suppressants, and tricyclic antidepressants) (Messerli and Frohlich 1979) or other treatable cause of hypertension, such as renal artery stenosis or pheochromocytoma.

Non-pharmacologic therapy of hypertension may be very helpful in preventing the use of medications or reducing their number and dosage when definitely needed (Joint National Committee on Detection 1984). Weight reduction by caloric restriction often results in a substantial decrease in blood pressure even if the ideal weight is not achieved. Moderate dietary sodium restriction is also helpful (MacGregor et al. 1982). Therefore, patients with essential hypertension should be given proper counseling for salt restriction. Heavy alcohol consumption may elevate the blood pressure (Klatsky 1982); therefore those who drink should do so only very moderately. Avoidance of smoking and a regular isotonic exercise program may be helpful. Behavior modification programs, including relaxation and biofeedback therapies, have shown modest but definite reductions in blood pressure.

In many situations drugs are needed for proper control of elevated blood pressure at rest and exercise. A wide choice of drugs is now available. Although antihypertensive medications may in some cases lead to sexual dysfunction, when properly selected for the individual patient, they may avoid such effects while controlling the blood pressure for safer performance of sexual activity.

For a successful program of blood pressure control, the professional must help the patient understand the significance of blood pressure and his or her participation in long-term followup and therapy. The patient must understand the condition and be motivated to work with the professional who, at the same time, must develop an attitude of positive approach and sensitivity to racial, cultural, and personal characteristics of the individual patient. Hypertension should be aggressively managed until blood pressure is returned to or near normal. When this is accomplished, no restriction need be placed on usual physical activities, including sexual relations. This, however, could be better evaluated by a stress exercise test and, whenever possible, by an ambulatory blood pressure recording, since the resting blood pressure in hypertensives does not accurately reflect the blood pressure during activity. In addition to evaluating the patient with an exercise test up to levels equivalent to the energy required during sexual activity, one should also consider the emotional factors, isometric effort, and Valsalva maneuver that may interplay during sexual activity (Papadopoulos 1981). The patient should be advised to avoid breath holding during coitus and to avoid sexual relations under hot and humid environmental conditions, after other strenuous activity, or while under emotional stress. Nitroglycerin is to be used sublingually, prophylactically, if the patient has associated angina.

The patient should be closely followed while he or she is being treated and a report in regard to untoward symptoms to medications should be solicited, since sexual dysfunction could be counterproductive to continued sexual relations and compliance with the treatment. It is imperative to get a good psychosexual history of the patient before starting the medications to prevent unnecessarily attributing the patient's symptoms to the drugs. Reduction in dosage of medication or substitution of an equally effective drug with a lesser potential effect on the sexual mechanism may be instituted. Vasodilator drugs, alpha-adrenergic blockers, and ACE inhibitors appear to be the least likely to produce such effects.

When the goal of normalizing blood pressure cannot be readily achieved without disturbing side effects, the physician could settle for something less, knowing that even partial control of blood pressure would substantially reduce the risk of future complications. Open communication with the patient is imperative. The quality of life for many is more important than the quantity.

BIBLIOGRAPHY

Beyer, J. C., Enos, W. F. 1977. "Obscure causes of death during sexual activity." *Med Asp of Hum Sex* 14:81–94.

Buell, J. C. 1984. "Hot reactors." *Masters in Card* 2:14–15.

Bulpitt, C. J., Dollery, C. T., Carne, S. 1976. "Change in symptoms of hypertensive patients after referral to hospital clinic." *Brit Med J* 38:121–28.

Fox, C. A., Fox, B. 1969. "Blood pressure and respiratory patterns during human coitus." *J Reprod Fert* 19:405–15.

Gifford, R. W. 1973. "Sexual expenditure in patients with hypertensive disease: Commentary." *Med Asp Hum Sex* 3:90.

Guevara, A. 1969. "Serum gonadotropin and testosterone levels in uremic males undergoing intermittent dialysis." *Metabolism* 18:1062–66.

Hogan, M. J., Wallin, J. D., Baer, R. M. 1980. "Antihypertensive therapy and male sexual dysfunction." *Psychosomatics* 21:234–37.

Howard, E. J. 1973. "Sexual expenditure in patients with hypertensive disease." *Med Asp Hum Sex* 3:82–92.

Joint National Committee on Detection. 1984. "Report of the Joint National Committee on detection, evaluation and treatment of high blood pressure." *Arch Intern Med* 144:1045–57.

Kannel, W. B. 1976. "Some lessons in cardiovascular epidemiology from Framingham." *Am J Cardio.* 37:269–82.

Kannel, W. B., Dawber, T. R. 1974. "Hypertension as an ingredient of a cardiovascular risk profile." *Br J Hosp Med* 11:508–23.

Klatsky, A. L. 1982. "The relationship of alcohol and the cardiovascular system." *Ann Rev Nutr* 2:51–71.

Levy, N. B. 1973. "Sexual adjustment to maintenance hemodialysis and renal transplantation: National survey by questionnaire: Preliminary report." *Trans Am Soc Artif Intern Organs* 19:138–43.

Lim, V. S., Auletta, F., Kathpalia, S. 1978. "Gonadal dysfunction in chronic renal failure: An endocrinologic review." *Dialysis and Transplantation* 7:896–907.

Littler, W. A., Honour, A. J., Sleight, P. 1974. "Direct arterial pressure, heart rate and electrocardiogram during human coitus." *J Reprod Fert* 40:321–31.

Lovas, J. G. L., Silver, M. D. 1984. "Coincident rupture of berry aneurysm and aortic dissection during sexual intercourse." *Arch Pathol Lab Med* 108:271–72.

MacGregor, G. A., Best, F., Cam, J. et al. 1982. "Double-blind randomized crossover trial of moderate sodium restriction in essential hypertension." *Lancet* 1:352–55.

Mann, S., Craig, M. W. M., Gould, B. A. et al. 1982. "Coital blood pressure in hypertensives." *Br Heart J* 47:84–89.

Masters, W. H., Johnson, V. E. 1966. *Human sexual response.* pp. 35, 174. Boston: Little & Brown.

Messerli, F. H., Frolich, E. D. 1979. "High blood pressure: A common side effect of drugs, poisons and food." *Arch Intern Med* 139:682–87.

Moss, H. B., Procci, W. R. 1982. "Sexual dysfunction associated with oral antihypertensive medication: A critical survey of the literature." *Gen Hosp Psych* 4:121–29.

Nemec, E. D., Mansfield, L., Kennedy, J. W. 1964. "Heart rate and blood pressure responses during sexual activity in normal males." *Am Heart J* 92:274–77.

Papadopoulos, C. 1980. "Cardiovascular drugs and sexuality." *Arch Intern Med* 140:1341–45.

_____. 1981. "Coital precautions for hypertensives." *Med Asp Hum Sex* 8:16, 83.

Paulson, G. W. 1982. "Headaches associated with orgasm." *Med Asp Hum Sex* 16:103–12.

Petrich, J., Holmes, T. H. 1977. "Life change and onset of illness." *Med Clin North Am* 61(4):825–38.

Rowland, M., Robert, J. 1982. "Blood pressure levels in persons 6–74 years: United States 1976–1980, Advance data." National Center for Health Statistics, Vital and Health Statistics No. 84. U.S. Dept. of Health and Human Services, Public Health Service.

Scott, J. C. 1930. "Systolic blood pressure fluctuations with sex, anger and fear." *J Comp Psychol* 10:97–114.

Ueno, M. 1963. "The so-called coition death." *Jap J Leg Med* 17:333–40.

6
Sex and the Stroke Patient

Each year, nearly 160,000 people die from stroke, but twice this number join the ranks of the approximately 2 million stroke survivors (American Heart Association 1988). With early and adequate rehabilitation measures and with prevention of complications, 60 to 80 percent of stroke victims will have the ability to ambulate alone and be independent for daily activities. An additional 10 to 25 percent can be expected to ambulate and perform activities of daily living with assistance. The ability to perform in competitive employment or in homemaking activities can be expected in 45 to 50 percent (Cohen 1979).

Stroke has usually been considered a condition of older people, but many cases occur at middle or earlier age. The National Health Interview Survey revealed that 43.4 percent of the strokes had occurred at age 20 to 65 years (Baum 1982). It has also been reported that the survival rate after a stroke is related to the patient's age (Baum and Robins 1981). Approximately 49 percent of patients age 65 years or younger survived for five years after the initial attack, but only 35 percent of the 65 to 74 year group and 22 percent of the 75 to 84 year group.

The predominance of stroke in older age and the myth that disabled people are asexual led to little emphasis on the sexual aspects of rehabilitation of stroke patients and often the feeling of many stroke survivors that their sex life is ended.

PHYSIOLOGIC AND PATHOLOGIC ASPECTS

Stroke leads to deficits of motion, loss of speech and communication, and impaired ability to receive sensory stimuli, all of which lead to discouragement, concern, and difficulties in sexual function and sexual rehabilitation. Sexual concerns of stroke survivors or their sexual partners are common. These concerns usually emerge after the patient is medically stable. Most physical recovery occurs within a few weeks after the stroke, and during this time emphasis is placed on improving motion, walking, activities of daily living, cognitive problems, and speech impairment. As recovery improves, attention shifts to interpersonal issues, such as socialization, recreation, and sexuality (Bray 1984).

In a report on the sexual behavior of 105 patients treated for a cerebrovascular accident (Kalliomaki, Markkanen and Mustonen 1961) whose age varied from 20 to 60 years, in most male patients a decrease in coital frequency occurred. The same phenomenon was observed in only half of the women. There was a decrease in libido, which was more common in right side paralysis than left side. Goddess and co-workers (1979) also found a greater incidence of impaired libido after left than right hemisphere stroke. Another study, however, (Monga, Lawson and Inglis 1986) showed no significant difference in the decline of sexual function between left- and right-sided lesions in men, and women with right-sided lesions had lesser decline in sexual function than women with left-sided lesions. Further discrepancy was added by another report (Coslett and Heilman 1986) based on 26 right-handed men who had a single hemispheric infarct with unilateral stroke. Their data revealed that the prevalence of major sexual dysfunction was significantly greater after right hemisphere stroke than after left. The authors concluded that their data are consistent with the hypothesis that the right hemisphere is dominant for sexual function.

A small series of interviews with 16 wives of stroke patients revealed that the sexual relationship was less satisfactory in 81 percent of the couples and the frequency of sexual relations became less in 75 percent (Malone 1975). Fifty percent of the wives expressed concern about the changes. In a reported study (Bray, DeFrank and Wolfe 1981) that investigated the sexual interest, function, and attitudes of 35 male and female patients, 79 percent of the men and 73 percent of the women reported sexual function to be of importance to themselves, while all of the men and 73 percent of the women believed it to be of importance to others of their age. However, the men experienced a significant decrease in the ability to achieve erection and to ejaculate, and all of the women who were premenopausal at the time of stroke reported major alterations in menses.

In a consecutive series of 51 stroke hemiplegics (Sjogren, Damber and Liliequist 1983), which consisted of 39 male and 12 female patients, it was revealed that 31 percent of the males and 27 percent of the females had stopped the foreplay, while 15 percent of males and 18 percent of the females had decreased the duration of the foreplay. Elimination of intercourse appeared to be more common in males than in females. Whereas 41 percent of males had stopped and 31 percent had decreased the frequency of sexual activity, only 17 percent of the females stopped and 42 percent had decreased the frequency. The duration of the whole sexual activity was decreased by the majority of males and nearly half of the females. However, few male patients had increased the duration of foreplay and of total sexual activity. Prior to stroke, 21 percent of the males, often or occasionally had difficulty achieving an erection. After the brain damage, the majority of these patients had such difficulties. The sexual drive toward the partner was decreased. In this study there was no difference in decreased libido, whether the lesion was in the dominant or the nondominant brain hemisphere. Among the females, 58 percent had orgasmic dysfunction before the stroke, but 75 percent of these patients had such dysfunction thereafter. The authors believe that hormonal disturbances or use of antihypertensive drugs were not the cause of sexual dysfunction and that the latter may rather be explained in terms of coping with their disease. In a study of the partnership adjustment and fulfillment of the same group of stroke patients (Sjogren 1983), retarded ejaculation occurred in 15 percent of the males after the stroke. The patients reported reduced sexual enjoyment due to erectile problems, fatigue, fear of relapse, reduced skin sensitivity, and orgasmic problems. After the stroke a marked reduction in levels of sexual fulfillment occurred among the males and some females.

Hawton (1984) reported on the sexual adjustment of 50 men, with mean age of 49 years, who had strokes. They were interviewed approximately six months after the incident. Interest in sex had returned in most cases, although the level of interest was reduced in some. Nearly all of the men had regained their erectile capacity, usually after a delay of approximately seven weeks after the stroke. Of those sexually active with their partner before the stroke, over half had resumed sexual intercourse by the time of the interview. Most of these men had encountered difficulty because of the physical consequences of their stroke, but two-thirds had tried new sexual positions to compensate for this. Whether or not a couple resumed sexual activity after the man's stroke was largely predictable on the basis of the frequency of their previous sexual activity, rather than the man's age or the severity of the physical disability.

Another study, however, (Monga, Lawson and Inglis 1986) based on 113 patients (78 men, 35 women) interviewed after a stroke at the one-year follow-up appointment in an outpatient clinic revealed significant decline in libido. The men had a significant decrease in the ability to achieve erection and to ejaculate. The mean age of the male patients was 68.6 years. Similarly, significant problems were reported by the women regarding vaginal lubrication and orgasm. Eighty-four percent of men and 60 percent of women enjoyed their sex lives before the stroke, as compared to only 30 percent of men and 31 percent of women after the stroke.

Three cases of hypersexuality and deviant sexual behavior have been reported (Monga et al. 1986). The premorbid sexual behavior of these patients during childhood and adult life was not known. Involvement of the temporal lobe, with lesions detected by computerized tomography, was the only common factor in all three cases.

EMOTIONAL AND PSYCHOLOGICAL ASPECTS

Sjogren (1983) reported that about half of the stroke patients felt they were less responsive to their partner's sexual initiatives. Half of the males and one-third of the females found the partner less responsive to sexual initiatives and less emotionally engaged than before the stroke. Stroke victims acknowledged that they had fewer thoughts of and showed less interest in mutual partnership sexuality. Sexual avoidance may be a sign of fear of sex and not of decreased desire. At times, changes and decrease in the sexual partnership drive may be an avoidance behavior because of the patient's previous dysfunction, or it may reflect frustration over the onset of increased sexual problems after the stroke. Reduced self-esteem may also play a role. The fact that patients have great difficulty in coping with major changes in their life-styles and are unable to perform according to their own expectations may lead to reduced self-esteem and frustrated sexual activity. Dependence on the spouse in the self-care of daily living may also affect the patient's sexuality since sexual and interpersonal aspects of a partnership are interwoven. Reduced somatic and mental capacity, loss of occupation, and fear of relapse make the patient a potential victim of a dependent sick role. At the same time the spouse may become overprotective and infantilize the disabled partner. Many patients, particularly females, believed that the decrease in sexual enjoyment was due to fatigue which, Sjogren (1983) felt, may be due to reactive depression that commonly occurs after stroke.

In a study of 91 stroke patients (Feibel and Springer 1982) the incidence of depression six months after the stroke was 26 percent. The depression was significantly correlated with failure to resume premorbid social activities. The authors found that the depression state was not significantly related to age, sex, marital or cognitive status, or side of brain involvement. They concluded that the health care team must carefully identify, monitor, and manage depression in the patient recovering from stroke. Furthermore, emotional distress, especially anxiety and frustration, are common problems after a stroke (Binder 1983). Other common difficulties include overdependence on others, inflexible thinking, impatience, irritability, impulsivity, denial and lack of awareness of problems, insensitivity to others, and poor social perception. Occasionally, suicidal ideation and paranoid delusions occur. Brain damaged patients may jump to conclusions after considering only part of the relative data. Such behavior often leads to the misinterpretation of others' emotions and erroneous conclusions. Impaired initiative and lack of empathy can contribute to insensitive, demanding behavior and a resulting breakdown of interpersonal relationships.

THE SPOUSE

In a study of the psychosocial readjustment of spouses of aphasic patients (Kinsella and Duffy 1979) the authors looked at the adjustment of three populations: spouses of aphasics only, hemiplegics with aphasia, and of hemiplegics alone. Their results indicated maladjustment for all groups; however, spouses of aphasics reported more loneliness, whereas spouses of hemiplegics reported more boredom. Spouses in all three groups implied reduced contact with friends, less social interaction, impaired leisure activity, and altered sexual relationships. Explanations given by healthy spouses for reduced coital frequency and altered sexual relations included, ". . . a general breakdown of the marriage, strong revulsion at the physical appearance of the patient, or fear that intercourse may promote another stroke."

Marron (1982) cautioned that rejection of the stroke patient by the spouse may reflect previous difficulties in the couple's relationship. He added that personality changes and laborious communication with the affected partner may strain the marriage.

ASSOCIATED DISEASES

The association of other diseases in the patient who develops a stroke should be seriously considered because of their pathophysiological and pharmacological effects on the patient. Many of these patients may suffer from hypertension, arteriosclerotic cardiovascular disease with impairment of peripheral vascular perfusion — including perfusion of the genitalia, anginal syndrome, previous myocardial infarction, and other cardiopulmonary conditions — or diabetes mellitus, all of which may independently affect their sexuality.

COUNSELING AND REHABILITATION

It is vital for the stroke victim to regain a sense of usefulness and independence, which can be achieved by repetitive training and preparing of the patient for the activities of daily life. The restoration of the stroke victim to self-sufficiency as soon as possible should be the goal. Speech therapy to help with language difficulties, physical therapy to deal with mobility impairment, psychotherapy and/or medications to deal with the emotional and mental problems of the patient are very important in the rehabilitative stage.

Reassurance and support from the physician and the health care team is vital and should involve the family, to impress upon them the necessity of giving much attention to the brain damaged family member. The goal of rehabilitation should be the capacity of the patient to return to family, vocational, recreational and, for the previously sexually active patient, sexual activities. The achievement of these goals will depend on the characteristics of the disease process, its nature, location and extent; on the premorbid personality strengths and weaknesses of the person, and the support system within the family and community.

It is recognized that the prognosis for ultimate functioning is related in inverse fashion to the time interval between the episode and the beginning of rehabilitation (Cohen 1979). Planning for long-term management should begin concurrently with acute medical management. Once the vital signs are stable and the patient is conscious, definitive rehabilitation measures should begin in most cases within a day or two after the onset. For most stroke patients a team of many health disciplines is needed. The physician, nurse, physical therapist, and occupational therapist are the most frequent team members. The social worker and the psychologist are also often involved. When necessary a speech pathologist and vocational specialist should be considered. Efforts to establish communication should start early. During the course of treatment the pattern of psychological response is assessed and with it the need for intervention. As attention is paid to the various needs of daily activity, one should consider that decreased physical mobility can necessitate changes in how intercourse is accomplished. Coital positioning presents a major problem for couples when one partner had a stroke, since most of the time the neurologic difficulty makes it virtually impossible for the male victim to assume the male superior position. Careful and sensitive instructions to the couple by the health professional are needed and may lead to rewarding and tension-relieving sexual success (McCormick, Riffer and Thompson 1986).

The attending physician and the rehabilitation nurse should deal early with the psychosocial, including the sexual, concerns of the patient. Sexual concerns and problems of post-stroke patients are of sufficient magnitude to deserve special attention. Sexual counseling is a natural component of the rehabilitation process. In one study (Sjogren 1983) extremely few patients were offered, or asked for, sexual counseling. It was felt that during the early phase denial may block the search for information and that the patient's depression and/or decreased self-esteem may lead to passivity, or that sexual taboos may inhibit even the most simple question about sexual matters. In another study (Goddess, Wagner and Silverman 1979), however, 24 of 25 subjects interviewed stated that they welcome open and frank discussion of their sexual needs, desires, and practices.

In a report on post-stroke sexuality (McCormick, Riffer and Thompson 1986), 37 wives of stroke patients who were interviewed were essentially unanimous in reporting a rather complete failure on the part of health professionals to educate them about their post-hospitalization roles as principal care givers and about post-stroke sexuality. Because the topic was not discussed, they assumed that sexual activities were frowned upon as an act that could cause another stroke. They hesitated to ask for sexual instructions because they considered this to be embarrassing and improper, although sexual activities had apparently been important to the couples prior to the stroke.

Medical and paramedical staff members must actively deal with the sexual problems of the stroke patient. Stroke patients are generally older people and sexual concerns of the elderly are rarely discussed. In addition, some health professionals' attitudes about age may include wishes to avoid personal involvement with these patients. In some cases, the health professional may become demoralized about the slowly recuperating patient and little communication about psychosocial and certainly sexual issues takes place (Goldberg 1983). A careful sexual history obtained from the patient and the spouse is very helpful in guiding further counseling. Participation of the spouse is important, since he or she has to have a good understanding of the patient's condition and since aphasia and cognitive deficits can severely affect the communication between spouses that is necessary for sexual encounters. Understanding and alleviating their fears and concerns provides a solid base for more comprehensive counseling. Both partners may fear that resumption of sexual activity can cause recurrence of stroke, and either of them may use this as an excuse to avoid relations that may have been unsatisfactory before the stroke. Some patients would take the risk of sexual activity that they may fear in order to avoid losing the spouse's love. Resumption of sexual relations is valuable from the psychological point of view. The benefits include the rebuilding of confidence, release of tensions, and resumption of warm personal feelings.

With reassurance and education, the obstacles for patients with visual field and sensory loss may be overcome. Stimuli should be presented to the intact visual field or sensory side of the body. For patients with motor problems, communication between spouses about comfortable positioning and the use of props, such as handles on the headboard, side rails, foot boards, or extra pillows usually prove effective. Different positions can facilitate sexual intercourse. There is no one normal position for sexual intercourse. The best normal position is the one that the partners find physically satisfactory. Patients should be advised to empty both bladder and bowels prior to sexual activity to avoid embarrassing accidents. The surroundings must insure privacy. There must be no need for haste and the partner should take advantage of those intimacies that have been previously helpful. The goal should be the best they can do.

At times impotence occurs in the male when the female has been the victim of a stroke, even if their pre-stroke sex life had been satisfactory. Fear of provoking another stroke or hurting the patient or the feeling that such activity is improper under the circumstances may play a role. In the case of impotence of the patient or the female patient's spouse, readjustment of sexual activity should be advised. Some patients can benefit from the reminder that sexual activity is more than just intercourse. It also involves relating to one another, verbal affection, kissing, and simple hugging. Stroke patients can still experience gratification and closeness, especially if they existed before the stroke.

BIBLIOGRAPHY

American Heart Association. 1988. "Heart Facts." Dallas: AHA Office of Communications.

Baum, H. M. 1982. "Stroke prevalence: An analysis of data from the 1977 National Health Interview Survey." *Publ Health Reports* 97:24–30.

Baum, H. M., Robins, M. 1981. "Survival and prevalence." *Stroke* 12:59–68.

Binder, L. M. 1983. "Emotional problems after stroke." *Curr Concepts of Cerebrovasc Dis* (Stroke) 18:17–21.

Bray, G. P. 1984. "Sexual function poststroke." *Med Asp of Hum Sex* 18:115–23.

Bray, G. P., DeFrank, R. S., Wolfe, T. L. 1981. "Sexual functioning in stroke survivors." *Arch Phys Med Rehab* 62:286–88.

Cohen, B. S. 1979. "Rehabilitation of the stroke patient." *MD State Med J* 28:82–83.

Coslett, H. B., Heilman, K. M. 1986. "Male sexual function: Impairment after right hemisphere stroke." *Arch Neurol* 43:1036–39.

Feibel, J. H., Springer, C. J. 1982. "Depression and failure to resume social activities after stroke." *Arch Phys Med Rehab* 63:276–78.

Goddess, E. D., Wagner, N. N., Silverman, D. R. 1979. "Poststroke sexual activity of CVA patients." *Med Asp of Hum Sex* 13:16–29.

Goldberg, R. L. 1983. "Sexual counseling for the stroke patient." *Med Asp of Hum Sex* 17:56A–56E.

Hawton, K. 1984. "Sexual adjustment of men who have had strokes." *J Psychosom Res* 28:243–49.

Kalliomaki, J. L., Markkanen, T. K., Mustonen, V. A. 1961. "Sexual behavior after cerebral vascular accident." *Fert & Sterl* 12:156–58.

Kinsella, G. J., Duffy, F. D. 1979. "Psychosocial readjustment in the spouses of aphasic patients: A comparative survey of 79 subjects." *Scand J Rehab Med* 11:129–32.

Malone, P. E. 1975. "A preliminary investigation of changes in sexual relations following stroke." In *Clinical aphasiology,* edited by R. H. Brookshire, pp. 175–83. Minneapolis: BRK.

Marron, K. R. 1982. "Sexuality with aging." *Geriatrics* 37:135–38.

McCormick, G. P., Riffer, D. J., Thompson, N. M. 1986. "Coital positioning for stroke afflicted couples." *Rehab Nursing* 11:17–19.

Monga, T. N., Lawson, J. S., Inglis, J. 1986. "Sexual dysfunction in stroke patients." *Arch Phys Med Rehab* 67:19–22.

Monga, T. N., Monga, M., Raina, M. S. et al. 1986. "Hypersexuality in stroke." *Arch Phys Med Rehab* 67:415–17.

Sjogren, K. 1983. "Sexuality after stroke with hemiplegia. II." *Scand J Rehab Med* 15:63–69.

Sjogren, K., Damberf, J. E., Liliequist, B. 1983. "Sexuality after stroke with hemiplegia. I." *Scand J Rehab Med* 15:55–61.

7
Cardiovascular Drugs and Sexuality

Several factors can affect the sexual function of a patient. The premorbid state of the individual, the physiopathologic effect of the disease process, the psychological state of the patient, the response of the marital partner to the illness, and the effects of treatment — particularly drugs — can play a role (Dengrove 1968). Since the drugs are only one variable in a complex system, the same substance may produce different sexual effects depending on the input of the other forces. Drugs may have a negative impact on the patient's quality of life as a result of possible adverse effects not only on sexuality but on the physical state, the emotional well-being, and the social and cognitive function. Sexual dysfunction may adversely affect the overall health of the individual, since sexuality is woven into the everyday life of most people and good sexual function is vital for emotional satisfaction (Levine 1976a).

Pharmacologic agents may affect the libido and the erectile and orgasmic phases of sexuality (Cooper 1969; Page 1975; Mills 1975; Shocket 1976; Levine 1976b). Adverse effects of drugs on sexual behavior have been considered to be of three types: sexual side effects of drugs, therapeutic effects of drugs on sexual dysfunction, and the use of drugs to control deviant or antisocial sexual behavior (Bancroft 1976). Most of the cardiovascular drug effects fall into the first category.

In general, the effects of drugs on male sexuality are far better described and understood than is their influence on the responses of females, partly because the male response is more visible and quantifiable (Kaplan 1974).

Most drugs have side effects of some sort or degree, depending on dosage, the unique reaction of each individual (their personality, age, sex, diet, underlying pathologic condition, and genetic factors), and the duration of drug consumption (Story 1974). Frequently, inadequate attention is paid to the sexual side effects of drugs.

While such psychological causes as interpersonal relationship deterioration, poor communication, and intrapsychic factors play a role in sexual dysfunction, disease processes, specific lesions, and pharmacologic agents can profoundly affect the sexual function (Levine 1976a). The emotional state of the patient, as well as the vascular, neurologic, and endocrine systems are involved in the integrity of normal sexual function. Understanding the anatomy and physiology of the sexual response clarifies in many situations the sexual effects of drugs (see Chapter 4 for review of the male response). In the female, the clitoris receives nerve and blood supply equivalent to that of the penis. Vasocongestive changes occur in the vagina equivalent to the erection phase of the male. They are again controlled by the parasympathetic system. Lubrication of the vaginal wall is also observed. During the orgasmic phase, contractions of the pelvic and perineal muscles occur, due to a spinal reflex center in the sacral area. Again, as in the male, the various stages are also under the influence of the higher central nervous system centers.

EFFECTS OF CARDIOVASCULAR DRUGS

Like other drugs, those used for cardiovascular diseases may affect the sexuality of the patient (The Medical Letter 1987; Seagraves et al. 1985). They may result in diminished libido, impotence, ejaculatory and orgasmic difficulties, inhibited vaginal lubrication, menstrual irregularities, and gynecomastia in men or painful breast enlargement in women. The incidence of reported side effects has varied. It is often difficult to document as reporting depends on information that some physicians are reluctant to pursue and patients may be embarrassed to volunteer. The method of collection of information has varied in various studies, from systematic use of written questionnaires, to oral questioning of the patient, to waiting for him or her to volunteer the information. An accurate incidence of sexual effects of many cardiovascular drugs is unavailable. The longer drugs have been used, the more observations have been made and information provided. Among the various cardiovascular medications, the antihypertensives have been studied more, possibly because of their widespread use and more common sexual side effects.

Cardiovascular drugs affect the neurogenic, hormonal, and vascular mechanisms. In a large study of 861 male patients receiving antihypertensive medications, 109 (12.6 percent) reported sexual dysfunction. In the same study the incidence of sexual dysfunction in 177 hypertensive control patients was 4 percent (Hogan et al. 1980). In another study (Bulpitt, Dollery and Carne 1976b) the incidence of impotence among untreated hypertensive men was 17.1 percent, compared with 6.9 percent of the normotensive men. Associated disease, such as peripheral and genital vascular disease may possibly play a role. However, it is more probable that telling someone that he or she has hypertension (labeling them) and the awareness of having this disease may lead to psychologic distress and lower psychologic well-being (Macdonald et al. 1985). Knowledge of the diagnosis of hypertension in an individual may lead that person to act in accordance with his or her perception of the limitations imposed by the disease; "the sick role" (Fletcher and Bulpitt 1985). However, treated patients still have higher incidence of sexual dysfunction (Bulpitt 1982). We believe that the effects of drugs can be properly evaluated if a good sexual history and evaluation of the quality of life of a hypertensive patient are obtained prior to medicating. The reported consequences of antihypertensive therapy have been so fragmentary and so unrelated to prior condition, other medications, alcohol intake, endocrine status, or condition of the partner that conclusions are difficult to draw (Korenman 1983).

In a review of 1,180 men in a medical outpatient clinic, 401 were found to be impotent and of the 188 who chose to be examined for their problem, it was felt that their dysfunction was due to medication in 25 percent of the cases. It was concluded that erectile dysfunction is a common and often overlooked problem in middle-aged men followed in a medical clinic (Slag et al. 1983).

In the largest group to date (5,485 patients), followed in the Hypertension Detection and Follow-up Program, sexually related side effects required discontinuation of treatment in 8.3 percent of male participants (Curb et al. 1985).

Several cardiovascular medications discussed here have more than one effect on the heart and more than one therapeutic use. Their sexual side effects are reviewed (see Table 2).

Diuretics

Thiazides and related compounds.

These compounds are among the most frequently used cardiovascular drugs. The group of thiazides and thiazide congeners, with which there were before only occasional cases of sexual dysfunction (Yendt, Guay and Garcia 1970; Keidan 1976; Materson 1978; PDR 1979, p. 1731), are now known to more commonly cause loss of libido and impotence.

Bulpitt and Dollery (1973) administered a questionnaire to 477 patients in a hypertensive clinic. Thirty-one percent of the men on diuretics alone complained of impotence. In a series of patients evaluated for sexual dysfunction after receiving antihypertensive medication, a positive history for this problem was found in 9 percent of the patients receiving hydrochlorothiazide alone (Hogan, Wallin and Baer 1980). In another report evaluating propranolol, methyldopa and captopril, more individuals also requiring a diuretic experienced sexual dysfunction and a substantial worsening of the general well-being over the duration of the study. This suggested that hydrochlorothiazide therapy may have a greater negative impact on the quality of life of hypertensive patients than captopril, propranolol or methyldopa alone (Williams et al. 1987). Cases of decreased libido and/or impotence associated with use of chlorthalidone have been reported (Stessman and Ben-Ishay 1980). The Medical Research Council Working Party report on mild to moderate hypertension (1981), revealed impotence as the most common adverse reaction to bendrofluazide treatment. There was an incidence of 16 percent impotence within three months, but the cases increased within one year. In most of those affected, impotence was reversible within a few weeks of stopping the bendrofluazide. Indapamide, a diuretic used for hypertension, has been described to cause impotence or reduced libido in less than 5 percent of cases (PDR 1987, p. 2020).

The explanation for impotence induced by thiazides has not been definite, but it could include the effect of thiazides on the vascular wall or the alternative possibility that zinc deficiency induced by diuretic agents that act on the first portion of the distal convoluted tubule may be responsible (Reyes, Olhaberry and Leary 1983). This could explain the lack of reported association with impotence of the loop diuretics, such as furosemide, which have not been shown to alter urinary zinc excretion in individuals with normal renal function. Kolodny (1979), however, stated that chronic use of these diuretics may also cause impotence.

TABLE 2
Sexual Effects of Cardiovascular Drugs

	Impotence	Ejaculation difficulties	Loss or decrease of libido	Gynecomastia	Menstrual irregularities	Breast enlargement in females
Thiazides and related comopunds	+	−	+	−	−	−
Spironolactone	+	−	+	+	+	+
Amiloride	+	−	±	−	−	−
Triamterene	+	−	−	−	−	−
Clonidine	+	±	−	+	−	−
Methyldopa	+	+	+	+	+	+
Guanabenz	+	−	±	+	−	−
Guanfacine	+	−	−	+	−	−
Reserpine	+	+	+	+	−	+
Ganglion blocking agents	+	+	−	−	−	−
Guanethidine	+	+	+	−	−	−
Guanadrel	+	+	+	−	−	−
Propranolol	+	−	+	−	−	−
Metoprolol	±	−	+	−	−	−
Timolol	+	−	+	−	−	−
Nadolol	+	−	+	−	−	−
Atenolol	+	−	+	−	−	−
Pindolol	+	−	+	−	−	−
Acebutolol	+	−	−	−	−	−
Labetalol	+	+	+	−	−	−

	Col 1	Col 2	Col 3	Col 4	Col 5	Col 6
Prazosin	±	−	−	−	−	−
Terazosin	±	−	−	−	−	−
Phenoxybenzamine	−	+	−	−	−	−
Hydralazine	±	−	+	−	−	−
Minoxidil	−	−	−	−	−	−
Pargyline	+	+	−	−	−	−
Captopril	±	−	−	−	−	−
Enalapril	±	−	−	−	−	−
Verapamil	+	−	−	+	+	+
Nifedipine	+	−	−	+	−	−
Diltiazem	±	−	−	+	+	−
Disopyramide	+	−	−	+	−	−
Mexiletine	+	−	+	−	−	−
Clofibrate	+	−	+	+	+	+
Probucol	+	−	±	−	−	−
Digitalis	+	−	+	+	−	+

− = no reported effect; + = reported effect; ± = possible or minimal reported effect

Thiazides may also inhibit vaginal lubrication and this has also been described with spironolactone (Semmens and Semmens 1978).

Potassium sparing diuretics.

Spironolactone's sexual side effects are impotence, (Spark et al. 1968; Brown et al. 1972; Greenblatt and Koch-Weser 1973b; Zarren and Black 1975), irregular menses (Spark et al. 1968; Brown et al. 1972; Levitt 1970), or amenorrhea (Levitt 1970), post-menopausal bleeding, and hirsutism. Decreased libido has also been reported (Spark et al. 1968; Zarren and Black 1975). Marked variation in the incidence of these side effects has been reported, but at usual clinical doses the incidence is less than 5 percent (McMahon 1978, pp. 144, 146). Gynecomastia, which is a fairly frequent complication, may be associated with mastodynia and is usually bilateral (Spark et al. 1968; Brown et al. 1972; Greenblatt and Koch-Weser 1973a, 1973b; Clark 1965; Mann 1963; Restifo and Farmer 1962; Smith 1962; Stokes 1962; Sussman 1963; Williams 1962). It may occur with dosages of 50 to 400 mg per day. Zarren and Black (1975) reported unilateral gynecomastia in patients receiving 50 mg per day. The incidence and extent of breast changes appear to be related to the dosage and the duration of therapy. Incidences of 100 percent and 0.4 percent have been reported (Spark et al. 1968; Greenblatt and Koch-Weser 1973a). Spironolactone's sexual side effects have been attributed to endocrine dysfunction (Loriaux et al. 1976).

Two other potassium sparing diuretics have slight sexual effects. Amiloride can cause impotence in 1 to 2 percent of cases (PDR 1987, p. 1319). Triamterene in a combination of hydrochlorothiazide has been reported to cause impotence in few patients (PDR 1987, p. 1914). We have also seen a few cases of this problem when taking the medication. The impotence improved upon discontinuation of the drug.

Centrally Acting Anti-Adrenergic Agents

Clonidine.

Clonidine hydrochloride reduces arterial pressure primarily through stimulation of hypothalamic and medullary alpha-receptors (Onesti et al. 1969; Finch 1975). Clonidine also slightly reduces heart rate, due in part to the increase in vagal tone. Activation of peripheral alpha-1 receptors, manifested by vasoconstriction and increased blood pressure is not usually evident with therapeutic oral doses (Drug Evaluations 1986, p. 516). Clonidine can cause drowsiness, sedation, and dryness of the mouth (Onesti et al. 1971). Incidence of impotence reported with Clonidine has varied. In a review of several studies it was 0 to 24 percent (Onesti et al. 1976). It has also been reported that retrograde ejaculation in men and inability to achieve orgasm in women can occur in patients treated with Clonidine (Abramowicz 1977a). Gynecomastia occurred in 0.5 percent of cases in one series (Onesti et al. 1971).

Sexual dysfunction could be due to the central sympatholytic action of the drug, its ability to produce drowsiness and sedation, or possible effects on parasympathetic and hormonal function (Mills 1975).

Methyldopa.

This antihypertensive medication depresses sympathetic nervous system activity by affecting the central nervous system. The action of methyldopa is believed to be associated with metabolism to alpha-methylnorepinephrine. This metabolite presumably lowers blood pressure by activating inhibitory alpha-adrenergic receptors of the brain, thereby reducing sympathetic outflow (Frohlich 1978). The most common side effects are lethargy, easy fatigability, and somnolence. Among other less common side effects, sexual difficulties and dysfunction occur. Possible mechanisms for this effect include the sedation and depression often associated with use of the drug. It has also been shown, however, that methyldopa increases the serum prolactin level, which may lead to sexual dysfunction (Turkington 1972; Frohman 1985). Some reports deny any notable change in libido, potency, or ejaculation (Bulpitt and Dollery 1973; Bauer et al. 1973). However, significant sexual side effects have been reported in other studies. In a review of 19 reports including 731 patients treated with methyldopa, McMahon (1978, p. 265) found a 1.3 percent incidence of impotence and 0.5 percent of failure to ejaculate. Johnson and co-workers (1966) reported a 2 percent impotence. However, Newman and Salerno (1974) reported that in 26 percent of their male patients treated with methyldopa for essential hypertension in a medical outpatient clinic, disorders of sexual function developed within a few days of beginning therapy. These disorders included decrease in libido, inability to maintain an erection, and difficulty in ejaculating. Within two weeks of discontinuing use of the drug and instituting a regimen of propranolol hydrochloride and hydralazine, these undesirable side effects had disappeared. Another report (Alexander and Evans 1975) stated an incidence of 53 percent erection failure among patients treated with methyldopa. In a study of the undesirable side effects of antihypertensive medications, Pillay (1976) reported on 30 patients treated with methyldopa and chlorthalidone, 24 of whom developed impotence. In this study sexual dysfunction was the most common side effect and caused a great deal of anxiety and many domestic problems.

The difference in the incidence of the side effects in various studies may be due to differences in methodology. In the studies with higher incidence, the information was specifically requested, verbally or by questionnaire. This higher level when information was specifically requested was also evident in the comparative study of Alexander and Evans (1975).

Breast enlargement, gynecomastia, and lactation have also been reported with methyldopa (PDR 1987, p. 1238). Some women reported loss of orgasm as well as decreased arousability (Kolodny 1979).

Guanabenz.

This antihypertensive medication is an orally active, central alpha-2 adrenoceptor agonist resulting in a decrease of sympathetic outflow from the brain at the bulbar level to the peripheral circulatory system. Like clonidine and methyldopa, guanabenz causes drowsiness and dry mouth in a sizable number of patients. Among the side effects occurring with a frequency of 3 percent or less are disturbances of sexual function and gynecomastia (PDR 1988, p. 2326).

Guanfacine.

This is a new centrally acting antihypertensive with alpha-2 adrenoceptor agonist properties. It also causes drowsiness and dry mouth, and among its other side effects impotence has been noticed in 1 to 4 percent depending on the dosage. Decrease of libido may also occur (PDR 1988, p. 1704).

Rauwolfia Alkaloids

Reserpine.

Reserpine is regarded as the prototype of the rauwolfia alkaloids and is the most commonly used drug in this group. Its anithypertensive effect has been attributed to depletion of catecholamine stores in peripheral sympathetic nerve terminals and the central nervous system, decreasing total peripheral resistance, heart rate, and cardiac output (Drug Evaluations 1986, p. 2591). Hyperprolactinemia is also induced by Reserpine (Turkington 1972; Frohman 1985). Mental depression occurs due to the central action of the rauwolfia alkaloids. In a cumulative review of many series, depression developed in 10 percent of patients treated with rauwolfia compounds (McMahon 1978, p. 346).

Decrease in libido, impotence, ejaculatory difficulties, gynecomastia, and breast enlargement in women may occur (Tuchman and Crumpton 1955; Bello and Turner 1956; Girgis et al. 1968; Drug Evaluations 1986, p. 520). The incidence of these side effects has varied from study to study. In a cumulative review of several reports, McMahon (1978, p. 346) found that decreased libido and erectile dysfunction occurred in approximately 1 percent of patients.

Ganglion Blocking Agents

These agents are rarely, if ever, used now. They act on autonomic ganglia to inhibit both sympathetic and parasympathetic function. Impotence may occur because of parasympathetic blockage and decreased emission, and failure of ejaculation can result from sympathetic blockage (Mills 1975).

Adrenergic Neuron Blockers

Guanethidine.

This is a strong antihypertensive medication, which for many years has been used for severe cases. It interferes with the release of norepinephrine from peripheral sympathetic nerve terminals. Once it gains access to the neuron it can cause depletion of norepinephrine stores within the nerve terminal. Guanethidine demonstrates effects similar to ganglion blocking drugs, but it does not demonstrate the additional effect of parasympathetic inhibition. In addition to orthostatic hypotension and increased frequency of bowel movements and diarrhea, it causes reduced emission, delay, or failure of ejaculation or retrograde ejaculation (Girgis et al. 1968; Moser 1974; Schinger and Gifford 1962; Bulpitt and Dollery 1973; Brahma et al. 1966; Prichard et al. 1968; Ruedy and Davies 1967; Eagan and Orgain 1961; Bauer et al. 1973; Oates et al. 1965). Potency is usually retained and orgasm may occur. Some patients, however, state that the sensation is attenuated (Page 1975). A number of patients experience loss of libido (Bauer et al. 1973) or impotence (Prichard et al. 1968; Ruedy and Davies 1967; Eagan and Orgain 1961; Bauer et al. 1973). A compilation of studies of patients treated with guanethidine disclosed that 52 percent had ejaculatory impairment and 31 percent had impotence (McMahon 1978, p. 194). Bauer and co-workers (1973) stated that permanent guanethidine induced damage, especially to the nerve fibers in the genital organs, as suggested by animal studies (Gerkens et al. 1971) has not been observed in humans. None of their 28 patients has had irreversible sexual failure after withdrawal of therapy with the drug.

Guanadrel.

This drug has a mechanism of action and hemodynamic effects similar to those of Guanethidine, though of shorter duration after withdrawal. It may cause less diarrhea and less orthostatic hypotension than Guanethidine and may also impair ejaculation to a lesser degree. The difference, however, may be slight (PDR 1987, p. 1552).

Beta-Adrenergic Blocking Agents

These drugs are being used as antihypertensives, anti-anginals, and anti-arrhythmics. They combine with the beta-adrenergic receptors located in the heart (beta-1) and on the arteries and arterioles of skeletal muscle, bronchi, pancreas, liver, kidney, and many other tissues (beta-2) blocking the response to sympathetic nerve impulses or circulating catecholamines. Beta-blocking agents differ in their relative affinity for beta-1 and beta-2 receptors. Propranolol, nadolol, timolol and pindolol are classified as "non-selective." Metoprolol, atenolol and acebutolol are more cardio-selective. Some beta-blocking drugs also have a partial agonist activity (intrinsic sympathomimetic activity), such as pindolol and acebutolol. These drugs also differ in the fact that some are more lipophilic agents (e.g., propranolol, metoprolol, pindolol) while others are more hydrophilic (e.g., atenolol, nadolol). Hydrophilic beta-blockers do not cross the blood brain barrier as readily as lipophilic agents and are thought to be less likely to cause central nervous system side effects (Drug Evaluations 1986, p. 467).

Possibly, beta-blocker induced sexual dysfunction is due to reduction of central sympathetic outflow, induction of sedation or depression, and decrease of genital blood flow due to peripheral vasoconstriction.

Propranolol.

This medication has been not only an effective antihypertensive, but also anti-anginal and anti-arrhythmic. The incidence of impotence has been reported as 4.7 percent in one series and 15 percent in another (Warren et al. 1976; Burnett and Chahine 1979). In the Veterans Administration Cooperative Study on antihypertensive agents (1977), of 81 patients treated with propranolol alone, impotence developed in 7.4 percent. Of the 77 patients treated with propranolol and hydrochlorothiazide, impotence developed in 14.2 percent. Erectile dysfunction usually occurs in dosages of 120 mg. or more per day (Warren, Brewer and Orgain; Warren and Warren 1977; Burnett and Chahine 1979). Two individual cases in which impotence developed with small dosages (40 to 60 mg. per day) of propranolol have been described (Knarr 1976; Miller 1976). The symptoms disappeared with discontinuation of the medication. Reduced libido has been reported in 2 to 5 percent of cases (Burnett and Chahine 1979; Hollilfield et al. 1976). Three patients have been described in whom Peyronie's disease developed during therapy with propranolol (Osborne 1977; Wallis, Bell and Sutherland 1977).

Metoprolol.

Like other lipophilic beta-blockers, it can cause mental depression and confusion. Reduced libido has occurred and there is potential for impotence (PDR 1987, p. 958). A case of Peyronie's disease in association with metoprolol has been reported (Yudkin 1977).

Timolol.

Decreased libido and impotence have also been described with this medication (PDR 1987, p. 1250). In a series of 509 patients with hypertension in whom timolol was used, impotence was reported in .8 percent (Attalla et al. 1981). It is interesting that sexual side effects have been described with the use of timolol in the form of eye drops, in cases of high intraocular pressure (McMahon et al. 1979; Fraunfelder and Meyer 1985).

Nadolol.

This hydrophilic beta-blocker that does not cross the blood brain barrier has also presented sexual side effects, but in rare cases. Loss of libido, impotence, and Peyronie's disease may occur (PDR 1987, p. 1575). In one study of nadolol in the treatment of hypertension of approximately 10,000 patients, the incidence of sexual dysfunction was reported as .3 percent (Jackson 1980). In a multicenter study with nadolol in hypertension, 60 cases of sexual disturbance were reported in a survey of 14,870 patients (Schimert and Buschbeck 1981). In a series of a total of 601 patients treated with nadolol for hypertension or angina, 6 patients developed impotence and decreased libido (Alexander et al. 1984).

Atenolol.

This is a cardioselective, hydrophilic beta-blocker, about which apparently few sexual side effects have been reported. In a series of 543 patients treated for hypertension with atenolol, one patient developed impotence (Zacharias et al. 1977). One instance of impotence was, however, recorded among 6 men who were being treated for hypertension (Douglas-Jones and Cruickshank 1976) and one patient in another series of 12 treated hypertensives (Ambrosioni et al. 1983). On the other hand, comparing the side effects of atenolol with those of a placebo, the incidence of impotence in a series of 482 patients was 2.8 percent in both groups (Zacharias 1980).

Pindolol.

This is a beta-blocker with partial agonist activity (intrinsic sympathomimetic activity). Impotence has been recorded among the various reactions that were seen in "2 percent or fewer patients" (PDR 1987, p. 1795). In a series of 1,200 patients who received pindolol for the treatment of hypertension, angina, and arrhythmias, "impotence occurred only rarely" (Gonasun and Langrall 1982). In a review of a European multicenter clinical trial of pindolol, the incidence of impotence was .03 percent (Rosenthal et al. 1979).

Acebutolol.

This is another beta-blocker with partial agonist activity. Impotence again was considered among the side effects that can occur in "2 percent or less" of patients using this medication (PDR 1987, p. 2197; Wahl et al. 1985).

Alpha- and Beta-Adrenergic Blocking Drugs

Labetalol.

This antihypertensive medication is a competitive antagonist at both alpha- and beta-adrenergic receptor sites. It selectively blocks alpha-1 receptors and is not selective in its action on beta receptors. Following short-term administration, the antihypertensive effect of labetalol is largely due to vasodilation; during prolonged oral therapy, both peripheral resistance and heart rate are reduced (Drug Evaluations 1986, p. 526). Decreased libido, impotence, and ejaculation failure may occur. The incidence has been 1 to 2 percent (PDR 1987, p. 986; Flamenbaum et al. 1985; Due, Giguere and Plachetka 1986).

Alpha-Adrenergic Blocking Drugs

Prazosin.

Prazosin, an antihypertensive, reduces total peripheral resistance by blocking alpha-1 adrenergic receptors. It dilates both arterioles and veins. Postural hypotension, dryness of the mouth, nasal congestion, and headache may occur and a .6 percent incidence of impotence was documented in a series of 934 patients (Pitts 1974). In another series of 100 hypertensive patients treated with prazosin, there was no documentation of impotence or loss of libido (Stokes et al. 1977). Brogden and co-workers (1977) stated that a major advantage of prazosin is its freedom from effects on sexual function. Stokes and Oates (1978) stated that the infrequency of sexual dysfunction, particularly failure of ejaculation, is notable.

The New Zealand Hypertension Study Group (1977) reported an incidence of .7 percent impotence necessitating withdrawal of prazosin. The Veterans Administration Cooperative Study Group on Antihypertensive Agents (1981), however, reported that sexual dysfunction was more frequently associated with prazosin than hydralazine.

Cases of priapism have also been related to prazosin therapy (Bhalla et al. 1979; Burke and Hirst 1980; Adams and Soucheray 1984).

Terazosin.

This is a new long-acting selective alpha-1 blocking agent that lowers blood pressure by reducing total peripheral resistance. In a report of the overall safety of terazosin as an antihypertensive agent, it was stated that impotence had a prevalence rate of less than 2 percent in both the terazosin-treated and the placebo-treated patients. The difference between the two treatment groups was not significant (Sperzel et al. 1986).

Phenoxybenzamine.

This vasodilator may now only occasionally be used in severe resistant hypertension cases (Drug Evaluations 1986, p. 530). This drug may inhibit emission and ejaculation, although erection and orgasm may be maintained (Mills 1975). In one report, four of seven patients who started receiving small doses of this medication experienced failure of ejaculation within a brief period (Green and Berman 1954). Potency and orgasm were intact. Moser and co-workers (1953) noted a decrease in the amount of seminal fluid in 34 percent of patients with vasospastic or occlusive disease who received this medication. Although it has been assumed that this drug produced retrograde ejaculation, an examination of post-orgasm urine samples suggested that retrograde ejaculation did not occur (Kedia and Persky 1981). Presumably, the drug may inhibit ejaculation by blocking alpha-adrenergic receptors that enervate the vas deferens, seminal vesicles, epididymis, and internal urethral sphincter.

Direct-Acting Vasodilators

Hydralazine.

This drug reduces the blood pressure by directly relaxing arteriolar smooth muscle; it has little effect on veins. Therefore, it is not surprising that there have been few reports implicating hydralazine as a cause of sexual dysfunction. One case of a hypertensive patient who was maintained on propranolol and furosemide was reported to have developed impotence after hydralazine was added, but it resolved when the medicine was discontinued (Ahmad 1980a). Another case of a patient on hydrochlorothiazide became impotent when 100 mg. of hydralazine was added to the regimen and the symptoms disappeared when the medicines were discontinued (Keidan 1976). In dosages above 200 mg. per day, approximately 5 to 10 percent of men reported decreased libido, sometimes accompanied by impotence (Kolodny 1979). Kolodny suggested that a syndrome resembling systemic lupus erythematosus or pyridoxine deficiency may play a role.

Minoxidil.

This is a more potent and longer acting vasodilator reducing total peripheral resistance. It is useful in refractory cases of hypertension. No sexual dysfunction has been reported, but very often the patient develops hypertrichosis, with elongation, thickening, and enhanced pigmentation of fine body hair. Breast tenderness has developed in less than 1 percent of patients (PDR 1987, p. 2054).

Monoamine Oxidase Inhibitors

Pargyline.

This drug is rarely used today. Its long-term administration has been shown to reduce norepinephrine release in response to preganglionic stimulation (Puig, Wakade and Kirpekar 1972). There is a reduction in the number and activity of beta-adrenergic receptors, as well as in the number of alpha-2 adrenergic and serotonergic receptor sites (Drug Evaluations 1986, p. 139). Disordered sexual func-tion, such as delay in ejaculation and impotence, has been reported (PDR 1987, p. 525).

Angiotensin-Converting Enzyme Inhibitors

Captopril and Enalapril.

These drugs cause decrease in circulating angiotensin II and aldosterone levels. They are vasodilators and have an antihypertensive effect associated with a decrease in total peripheral resistance. They also decrease the venous tone. They are both thought not to cause sexual dysfunction (The Medical Letter 1987). Rare cases of impotence may occur with enalapril (PDR 1987, p. 1348) and captopril (Croog et al. 1986).

In a multicenter study of 626 white men with mild to moderate hypertension, the effects of captopril, methyldopa and propranolol on the quality of life was studied (Croog et al. 1986). Four hundred eighty-six patients had a 24-week followup on their quality of life. Among those who did not finish the study the most common adverse reaction was fatigue or lethargy, followed by sexual disorder, headache, and sleep disorder. Sexual function evaluated included sexual desire, problems with erection, and problems of ejaculation. In 24 weeks, the captopril group was better off than the methyldopa group in terms of the measures of general well-being, physical symptoms and sexual dysfunction, cognitive function, work performance and satisfaction with life. The captopril group differed from the propranolol group in regard to various measures, with better general well-being and less sexual dysfunction.

Calcium-Channel Blocking Agents

This group of drugs inhibits the entry of calcium into cardiac cells and smooth muscle cells of the coronary and systemic vasculature. These agents are useful in a number of cardiovascular disorders, including hypertension, angina, and arrhythmias. Not much information is available about their sexual side effects.

Verapamil.

This medication has been found to cause hyperprolactinemia, and a case of galactorrhea in a young female patient treated for atrial tachycardia has been reported (Gluskin, Strasberg and Shah 1981). Among the adverse reactions of Verapamil reported in less than 1 percent of patients are gynecomastia, spotty menstruation, and impotence (PDR 1987, p. 1878). In a series of 14 male patients treated with verapamil for atrial arrhythmias, impotence developed in three (King, Pitchon and Stern 1983).

Fearrington and colleagues (1983) detected hyperprolactinemia in six and galactorrhea in three of the seven women who were being treated with verapamil. None of these patients developed amenorrhea, which "may be a diagnostic point in support of verapamil hyperprolactinemia-galactorrhea as opposed to other causes of this syndrome." The Division of Epidemiology and Surveillance within the U.S. Food and Drug Administration received 18 reports of gynecomastia occurring during verapamil therapy. During the same period, however, 13.5 million prescriptions for verapamil were dispensed (Tanner and Bosko 1988).

Nifedipine.

This calcium blocker may cause "sexual difficulties," which may occur in 2 percent or less of patients (PDR 1987, p. 1563). In a small series of patients that included 14 men being treated for angina, which studied the effects of placebo, nifedipine and propranolol, approximately half of the patients developed impotence on nifedipine or propranolol and 27 percent on placebo (Dargie et al. 1981). Eleven cases of gynecomastia related to nifedipine were recently reported (Tanner and Bosko 1988).

Diltiazem.

"Sexual difficulties" are reported among the adverse reactions occurring in less than 1 percent of cases (PDR 1987, p. 1174). One case of gynecomastia with diltiazem therapy has been reported (Tanner and Bosko 1988).

Anti-arrhythmics

Disopyramide.

Disopyramide is an effective anti-arrhythmic drug, especially for ventricular arrhythmias. It resembles quinidine and procainamide in its effects on the heart, but it is chemically distinct (Abramowicz 1977b). It has anticholinergic effects, which include urinary retention, dry mouth, blurring of vision, constipation, and aggravation of glaucoma. In clinical trials with 1500 patients, impotence was reported in 1 to 3 percent of the cases (PDR 1987, p. 1891). McHaffie and colleagues (1977) reported a case of a 47-year-old man in whom impotence developed when the plasma concentration of the drug was 14 ng/ml. There was full recovery of sexual function when dose adjustments lowered the concentration to 3 ng/ml. There was also a case of a 35-year-old man who developed impotence after three weeks of disopyramide therapy for premature ventricular beats. Full recovery of sexual function occurred a few days after discontinuation of the medicine, with recurrence of impotence when it was restarted (Ahmad 1980b).

Mexiletine.

Apparently this new, Class I-B anti-arrhythmic medication can cause impotence and decreased libido. They are reported in the adverse reactions occurring in less than 1 percent (PDR 1987, p. 716).

Hypolipidemics

Clofibrate.

This is one of the first hypolipidemic agents. In addition to gastrointestinal symptoms, hepatic and renal dysfunction and sexual side effects may occur (PDR 1987, p. 634). Breast tenderness or enlargement has been noted in 5.2 percent and decreased libido or impotence in 14.1 percent of the 1,065 patients treated with clofibrate in the Coronary Drug Project (The Coronary Drug Project Research Group 1975). In that study, the most common problem mentioned by patients receiving clofibrate, in comparison with placebo patients, was decreased libido or impotence. Schneider and Kaffarnik (1975) reported three cases among approximately 100 patients who had been receiving clofibrate therapy and in whom impotence developed within one year after commencement of treatment with this drug. Two of the patients had previously suffered a myocardial infarction. Two patients observed improvement of the symptoms three and four weeks after interruption of clofibrate therapy; one patient again became impotent when clofibrate was resumed. The third patient continued taking the drug and the impotence persisted. The mechanisms involved in the sexual dysfunction are not clear and require further study. Clofibrate may induce alterations in the degradation of endogenous androgenic steroids or in predisposed patients may compete for albumin binding sites and thus lead to deprivation of androgens after some weeks (Schneider and Kaffarnik 1975).

Probucol.

This is another hypolipidemic that lowers serum cholesterol. The most common adverse reactions are gastrointestinal symptoms, eosinophilia, and occasionally an idiosyncratic reaction. Impotence has occurred in rare cases (PDR 1987, p. 1358).

Digitalis

Estrogen-like effects are occasionally seen with digitalis over long periods of time, probably due to its chemical similarity to sex hormones (LeWinn 1953). Most post-menopausal women who have been receiving digitalis for more than two years show maturation of the vaginal squamous epithelium (Navab, Koss and LaDue

1965). Gynecomastia is an infrequent but well-recognized side effect in men (LeWinn 1953) and enlargement of the mammary glands may occur in women. Neri and co-workers (1980) investigated the effect of digoxin on sexual function. The study group consisted of 14 patients who had been on digoxin for a long time. Members of the control group were of similar cardiac functional capacity and age (25 to 40 years) and were randomly selected from rheumatic heart disease patients. Personal interviews and a questionnaire were used to evaluate sexual behavior. Five of the 14 patients who were taking digoxin experienced lack of sexual desire and complete erectile dysfunction. The authors felt that plasma estrogen levels, which are higher under long-term administration of digoxin, antagonize both the peripheral and central stimulation of androgens, an action that is assumed to depress libido and impair erectile response.

BENEFICIAL EFFECTS OF CARDIOVASCULAR DRUGS ON SEXUALITY

The prophylactic use of beta-blockers and sublingual nitrates by coronary patients to prevent angina during intercourse has been recommended and proven beneficial (Hellerstein and Friedman 1970; Jackson 1978). A case of good response of atherosclerotic impotence to nitrates has also been reported (Mudd 1977).

Amyl nitrate is a vasodilator that has been prescribed in the past to relieve angina pectoris. As reported (Hollister 1975; Cohen 1979), it has become a popular sex drug among some groups who claim that the drug enhances the intensity and pleasure of orgasm. There are no scientifically valid data to substantiate its aphrodisiac effects.

Anti-arrhythmic drugs have been beneficial in preventing arrhythmias induced by sexual activity and also in reducing the concern of patients with palpitations during intercourse (Regestein and Horn 1978). When properly selected, antihypertensive medications, by controlling the blood pressure of hypertensive patients, may allow a better quality of life with fewer symptoms secondary to the hypertensive response to the sexual activity.

THERAPEUTIC CONSIDERATIONS

In evaluating the factors of sexual dysfunction of the cardiovascular patient, the impact of drugs should be considered. Cardiovascular drugs may affect the sexuality of the patient through their effects on the central and peripheral nervous system, the vascular system, and hormonal changes.

Pharmacologic agents may impair the libidinal, erectile, and orgasmic phases of the human sexual response. Incidences of adverse sexual effects of drugs are difficult to document. Reporting depends on information that some physicians are reluctant to pursue and patients may be embarrassed to volunteer (Abramowicz 1977a). Knowledge of these side effects is vital for sexual counseling of the cardiovascular patient.

Proper evaluation of the quality of life in hypertensive patients should be made before subjecting them to therapeutic risks (Pickering 1975). Tactful evaluation of the sexual function of the patient before prescribing medications with potential side effects is advisable and may prevent later unnecessary discontinuation of therapy with these medications. This is of importance since impotence has been more frequent in untreated hypertensive men compared with normotensive men (Bulpitt, Dollery and Carne 1976). Chatterjee (1987) believed that patients with asymptomatic hypertension may also suffer from psychological side effects, which result not only from antihypertensive therapy, but also from the patients' knowledge that their high blood pressure may predispose them to serious cardiovascular complications. Loss of self-image and reactive depression may occur.

The health professional may, by inquiring in a comfortable and caring manner about the sexual function of the patient during treatment, discover the effect of drugs. Telling the patient that a drug can cause impotence may indeed cause it, independent of the drug's actual effect (Scheingold and Wagner 1974). Fear of being impotent is often a major cause of impotence. Once a sexual problem is discovered, an evaluation of its nature and then its cause (organic or psychic) is vital. The patient's compliance with the medication regimen may easily be affected because of the drug's effect on the sexuality of the patient. Among the several causes of noncompliance, sexual dysfunction should always be considered. In some situations, the patient may attribute his or her sexual problems to the heart or vascular disease and the anxiety may increase. Patients should always be encouraged to contact their physicians if they experience any side effects.

In an ideal drug regimen, the demand for maintenance of quality of life and for therapeutic effectiveness can be reconciled. By giving appropriate weight to quality of life measures, physicians will not only address the needs and concerns of their patients, but they may also expect that fewer patients with hypertension will fail to adhere adequately to their prescribed regimens or will withdraw from treatment (Croog et al. 1986).

From his own experience as a psychologist and sexual counselor Murphy (1978) suggests the following:

1. Avoid suggesting to the patient that antihypertensives cause sexual dysfunction.
2. Inquire about side effects in an interested, but casual way.
3. Refrain from using the word "impotence," if possible.
4. Be supportive and optimistic if the patient has a negative reaction to medication.
5. Avoid offering a clear cut choice between medication and sexual enjoyment.
6. Deal with sexual dysfunction promptly.
7. Refer the patient to a sex counselor, if necessary.

Sexual dysfunction, whether due to drugs or other factors, has an undesirable impact on marital relations. It may cause strain and impair the emotional relationship of the partners (Levine 1976a; Papadopoulos et al. 1980). A reduction in the dosage of medications or substitution of an equally effective drug with a lesser potential effect on the sexual mechanisms may be instituted. When the goal of normalizing the blood pressure cannot be readily achieved without disturbing side effects, the physician can be encouraged to settle for something less, knowing that even partial control of blood pressure would substantially reduce the risk of future complications (Freis 1975). The quality of life, for many, is more important than the quantity.

BIBLIOGRAPHY

Adams, J. W., Soucheray, J. A. 1984. "Prazosin-induced priapism in a diabetic." *J Urol* 132:1208.

Abramowicz, M. 1977a. "Clonidine (catapres) and other drugs causing sexual dysfunction." *Med Lett Drugs Ther* 19:81–82.

____. 1977b. "Dysopyramide (Norpace) for ventricular arrhythmias." *Med Lett Drugs Ther* 19:101–02.

Ahmad, S. 1980a. "Hydralazine and male impotence." *CHEST* 78:358.

____. 1980b. "Disopyramide and impotence." *Southern Med J* 73:958.

Alexander, J. C., Christie M. H., Vernam, K. A. et al. 1984. "Long-term experience with nadolol in treatment of hypertension and angina pectoris." *Am Heart J* 108:1136.

Alexander, W. D., Evans, J. I. 1975. "Side effects of methyldopa." *Brit Med J* 2:501.

Ambrosioni, E., Costa, F. V., Montebugnoli, L. et al. 1983. "Comparison of antihypertensive efficacy of Atenolol, Oxprenolol and Pindolol at rest and during exercise." *Drugs* 25 (Suppl. 2):30–36.

American Medical Association. 1986. *Drug Evaluations.* 6th ed. Chicago: American Medical Association.

Attalla, F. M., Saheb, I. V. H., Randall, R. F. et al. 1981. "Timolol-Blocadren post marketing surveillance program in hypertension." *Curr Ther Res* 29:423.

Bancroft, J. H. J. 1976. "Evaluation of the effects of drugs on sexual behavior." *Br J Clin Pharmacol* 3 (Suppl. 1):83–90.

Bauer, G. E., Hull, R. D., Stokes, G. S. et al. 1973. "The reversibility of side effects of guanethidine therapy." *Med J of Australia* 1:930–33.

Bello, C. T., Turner, L. W. 1956. "Reserpine as an antihypertensive in the outpatient clinic: A double-blind clinical study." *Am J Med Sci* 232:194–97.

Bhalla, A. K., Hoffbrand, B. I., Phatak, P. S. et al. 1979. "Prazosin and priapism." *Brit Med J* 2:1039.

Brahma, S. K., Chowdhury, B., Sarkar, B. K. et al. 1966. "Guanethidine in hypertension." *J Ind Med Assoc* 46:541–43.

Brogden, R. N., Heel, R. C., Speight, T. M. et al. 1977. "Prazosin: A review of its pharmacological properties and therapeutic efficacy in hypertension." *Drugs* 14:163–97.

Brown, J. J., Daries, D. L., Ferriss, J. B. et al. 1972. "Comparison of surgery and prolonged spironolactone therapy in patients with hypertension, aldosterone excess and low plasma renin." *Br Med J* 2:729–34.

Bulpitt, C. J. 1982. "Quality of life in hypertensive patients." In *Hypertensive cardiovascular disease: Pathophysiology and treatment,* edited by A. Amery, pp. 929–48. Norwell, Mass.: Martinus Nijhoff.

Bulpitt, C. J., Dollery, C. T. 1973. "Side effects of hypotensive agents evaluated by a self-administered questionnaire." *Br Med J* 3:485–90.

Bulpitt, C. J., Dollery, C. T., Carne, S. 1976. "Change in symptoms of hypertensive patients after referral to hospital clinic." *Br Heart J* 38:121–28.

Burke, J. R., Hirst, G. 1980. "Priapism and prazosin." (Letter) *Med J of Australia* 1:382.

Burnett, W. C., Chahine, R. A. 1979. "Sexual dysfunction as a complication of propranolol therapy in men." *Cardiovasc Med* 4:811–15.

Chatterjee, M. B. 1987. "Antihypertensive drug therapy and quality of life." *Quality of Life and Cardiovascular Care* 3:73–86.

Clark, E. 1965. "Spironolactone therapy and gynecomastia." *JAMA* 193:163–64.

Cohen, S. 1979. "The volative nitrites." *JAMA* 241:2077–78.

Cooper, A. J. 1969. "Factors in male sexual inadequacy: A review." *J Nerv Ment Dis* 149:337–59.

The Coronary Drug Project Research Group. 1975. "Clofibrate and niacin in coronary heart disease." *JAMA* 231:360–81.

Croog, S. H., Levine, S., Testa, M. A. et al. 1986. "The effects of antihypertensive therapy on the quality of life." *New Eng J of Med* 314:1657–64.

Curb, J. D., Borhani, N. O., Blaszkowski, T. P. et al. 1985. "Long-term surveillance for adverse effects of antihypertensive drugs." *JAMA* 253:3263–68.

Dargie, H. J., Lynch, P. G., Krikler, D. M. et al. 1981. "Nifedipine and propranolol: A beneficial drug interaction." *Am J of Med* 71:676–82.

Dengrove, E. 1968. "Sexual responses to disease processes." *J Sex Res* 4:257–66.

Douglas-Jones, A. P., Cruickshank, J. M. 1976. "Once-daily dosing with atenolol in patients with mild or moderate hypertension." *Br Med J* 1:990–91.

Due, D. L., Giguere, G. C., Plachetka, J. R. 1986. "Postmarketing comparison of labetalol and propranolol in hypertensive patients." *Clin Ther* 8:624–31.

Eagan, J. T., Orgain, E. S. 1961. "A study of 38 patients and their responses to guanethidine." *JAMA* 175:550–53.

Fearrington, E. L., Rand, C. H., Rose, J. D. 1983. "Hyperprolactinemia-galactorrhea induced by verapamil." *Amer J Cardiol* 51:1466–67.

Finch, L. 1975. "The central hypotensive action of clonidine and BAY 1470 in cats and rats." *Clin Sci Mol Med* 48 (Suppl.):273–76.

Flamenbaum, W., Weber, M. A., McMahon, F. G. et al. 1985. "Monotherapy with labetalol compared with propranolol." *J Clin Hypertens* 1:56–69.

Fletcher, A., Bulpitt, C. J. 1985. "The treatment of hypertension and quality of life." *Quality of Life and Cardiovascular Care* 1:140–50.

Fraunfelder, F. T., Meyer, S. M. 1985. "Sexual dysfunction secondary to topical ophthalmic timolol." *JAMA* 253:3092–93.

Freis, E. D. 1975. "How far should blood pressure be lowered in treating hypertension?" *JAMA* 232:1017–18.

Frohman, L. A. 1985. "The anterior pituitary." In *Cecil Textbook of Medicine,* edited by J. B. Wyngaarden & L. H. Smith. pp. 1263–64. Philadelphia: W. Saunders.

Frolich, D. E. 1978. "Newer concepts in antihypertensive drugs." *Prog Cardiovasc Dis* 20:385–402.

Gerkens, T., Mashford, M. L., Gannon, B. J. et al. 1971. "Prolonged effect of chronic guanethidine treatment on the sympathetic innervation of the genitalia of male rats." *Med J of Australia* 2:207–08.

Girgis, S. M., Etriby, A., El-Hefnawy, H. et al. 1968. "Aspermia: A survey of 49 cases." *Fertil & Steril* 19:580–88.

Gluskin, L. E., Strasberg, B., Shah, J. H. 1981. "Verapamil-induced hyperprolactinemia and galactorrhea." *Ann of Int Med* 95:66–67.

Gonasun, L. M., Langrall, H. 1982. "Adverse reactions to pindolol administration." *Am Heart J* 104:482–86.

Green, M., Berman, S. 1954. "Failure of ejaculation produced by dibenzyline." *Conn State Med J* 18:30–33.

Greenblatt, D. J., Koch-Weser, J. 1973a. "Adverse reactions to spironolactone." *JAMA* 225:40–43.

———. 1973b. "Gynecomastia and impotence: Complications of spironolactone therapy." *JAMA* 223:82.

Hellerstein, H. K., Friedman, E. H. 1970. "Sexual activity and the postcoronary patient." *Arch Intern Med* 125:987–99.

Hogan, M. J., Wallin, J. D., Baer, R. M. 1980. "Antihypertensive therapy and male sexual dysfunction." *Psychosomatics* 21:234–37.

Hollifield, J. W., Sherman, K., Zwagg, R. V. et al. 1976. "Proposed mechanisms of propranolol's antihypertensive effect in essential hypertension." *N Engl J Med* 295:68–73.

Hollister, L. E. 1975. "Drugs and sexual behavior to man." *Life Sciences* 17:661–67.

Jackson, D. A. 1980. "Nadolol, a once daily treatment for hypertension — Multi-centre clinical evaluation." *Brit J Clin Pract* 34:211–21.

Jackson, G. 1978. "Sexual intercourse and angina pectoris." *Br Med J* 2:16.

Johnson, P., Kitchin, A. H., Lowther, C. P. et al. 1966. "Treatment of hypertension with methyldopa." *Brit Med J* 1:133–37.

Kaplan, H. S. 1974. *The new sex therapy.* p. 87. New York: Brunner/Mazel.

Kedia, K. R., Persky, L. 1981. "Effect of phenoxybenzamine (Dibenzyline) on sexual function in man." *Urology* 18:620–22.

Keidan, H. 1976. "Impotence during antihypertensive treatment." *Can Med Assoc J* 114:874.

King, B. D., Pitchon, R., Stern, E. H. 1983. "Impotence during therapy with verapamil." *Arch Intern Med* 143:1248–49.

Knarr, J. W. 1976. "Impotence from propranolol?" *Ann Int Med* 85:259.

Kolodny, R. C. 1979. "Drugs and sex." In *Textbook of Sexual Medicine.* p. 324. Boston: Little, Brown & Co.

Korenman, S. G. 1983. "Clinical assessment of drug-induced impairment of sexual function in men." *CHEST* 83:391–92.

Levine, S. B. 1976a. "Marital sexual dysfunction: Introductory concepts." *Ann Intern Med* 84:448–53.

____. 1976b. "Marital sexual dysfunction: Erectile dysfunction." *Ann Intern Med* 85:342–50.

Levitt, J. I. 1970. "Spironolactone therapy and amenorrhea." *JAMA* 211:2014–15.

LeWinn, E. B. 1953. "Gynecomastia during digitalis therapy: Report of eight additional cases with liver function studies." *New Eng J Med* 248:316–20.

Loriaux, D. L., Menard, R., Taylor, A. et al. 1976. "Spironolactone and endocrine dysfunction." *Ann Intern Med* 85:630–36.

Macdonald, L. A., Sackett, D. L., Haynes, R. B. et al. 1985. "Hypertension: The effects of labeling on behavior." *Quality of Life and Cardiovascular Care* 1:129–39.

Mann, N. M. 1963. "Gynecomastia during therapy with spironolactone." *JAMA* 184:778–80.

Materson, B. et al. 1978. "Dose response to chlorthalidone in patients with mild hypertension." *Clin Pharmacol Ther* 24:192–98.

McHaffie, D. J., Guz, A., Johnston, A. 1977. "Impotence in patient on disopyramide." *Lancet* 1:859.

McMahon, C. D., Shaffer, R. N., Hoskins, H. D. et al. 1979. "Adverse effects experienced by patients taking timolol." *Amer J of Ophth* 88:736–38.

McMahon, F. G. 1978. *Management of essential hypertension.* New York: Futura Publishing.

The Medical Letter. 1987. "Drugs that cause sexual dysfunction." 29:65–68.

Medical Research Council Working Party on Mild to Moderate Hypertension. 1981. "Adverse reactions to bendrofluazide and propranolol for the treatment of mild hypertension." *Lancet* 2:539–43.

Miller, R. A. 1976. "propranolol and impotence." *Ann Int Med* 85:682–83.

Mills, L. C. 1975. "Drug-induced impotence." *Am Fam Physician* 12:104–06.

Moser, M. 1974. "Treatment of hypertension — A pragmatic approach." *Prev Med* 3:328–33.

Moser, M., Prandoni, A. G., Orison, J. A. et al. 1953. "Clinical experience with sympathetic blocking agents in peripheral vascular disease." *Ann Int Med* 38:1245–46.

Mudd, J. W. 1977. "Impotence responsive to glyceryl trinitrate." *Am J Psych* 134:922–25.

Murphy, R. J. 1978. "Compliance dilemma: Antihypertensives and sexual dysfunction." *Behav Med* 5:10–14.

Navab, A., Koss, L. G., LaDue, J. S. 1965. "Estrogen-like activity of digitalis." *JAMA* 194:142–44.

Neri, A., Aygen, M., Zukerman, Z. et al. 1980. "Subjective assessment of sexual dysfunction of patients on long-term administration of digoxin." *Arch of Sex Behav* 9:343–47.

New Zealand Hypertension Study Group. 1977. "Initial experience with prazosin in New Zealand." *Med J of Australia* (Spec. Suppl.) 2:23–26.

Newman, R. J., Salerno, H. R. 1974. "Sexual dysfunction due to methyldopa." *Brit Med J* 4:106.

Oates, J. A., Seligmann, A. W., Rousseau, P. et al. 1965. "The relative efficacy of guanethidine, methyldopa and pargyline as antihypertensive agents." *N Eng J Med* 273:729–34.

Onesti, G., Bock, K. D., Heimsoth, V. et al. 1971. "Clonidine: A new antihypertensive agent." *Am J Cardiol* 28:74–83.

Onesti, G., Martinez, E. W., Fernandes, M. 1976. "Alpha-methyldopa and clonidine: Antihypertensive agents with action on the central nervous system." In *The spectrum of antihypertensive drug therapy,* edited by G. Onesti and T. D. Lowenthal, p. 61. New York: Biomedical Information Corp.

Onesti, G., Schwartz, A. B., Kim, K. E. 1969. "Pharmacodynamic effects of a new antihypertensive drug catapres (ST-155)." *Circulation* 39:219–28.

Osborne, D. R. 1977. "propranolol and Peyronie's disease." *Lancet* 1:1111.

Page, L. B. 1975. "Advising hypertensive patients about sex." *Med Asp Hum Sex* 9:103–04.

Papadopoulos, C., Larrimore, P., Cardin, S. et al. 1980. "Sexual concerns and needs of the postcoronary patient's wife." *Arch Intern Med* 140:38–41.

Physicians' Desk Reference "PDR]. 1979. 33rd ed. Oradell, New Jersey: Medical Economics Co.

___. 1987. 41st ed. Oradell, New Jersey: Medical Economics Co.

___. 1988. 42d ed. Oradell, New Jersey: Medical Economics Co.

Pickering, G. 1975. "Assessing the quality of life in hypertensive patients under treatment." In *Hypertension — Its nature and treatment. CIBA International Symposium, Malta,* pp. 117–19. Horsham, Sussex: Ciba Laboratories.

Pillay, V. K. G. 1976. "Some side effects of alpha-methyldopa." *S Afr Med J* 50:625–26.

Pitts, N. E. 1974. "The clinical evaluation of prazocin hydrochloride, a new antihypertensive agent." In *Prazocin-evaluation of a new antihypertensive agent. Proceedings of a symposium,* edited by D. W. K. Cotton, pp. 149–63. Amsterdam: Excerpta Media.

Prichard, B. N. C., Johnston, A. W., Hill, I. D. et al. 1968. "Bethanidine, guanethidine and methyldopa in treatment of hypertension: A within-patient comparison." *Brit Med J* 1:135–44.

Puig, M., Wakade, A. R., Kirpekar, S. M. 1972. "Effect on the sympathetic nervous system of chronic treatment of pargyline and L-dopa." *J Pharmac Exp Ther* 182:130–34.

Regestein, Q. R., Horn, H. R. 1978, "Coitus in patients with cardiac arrhythmias." *Med Asp Hum Sex* 12:108–21.

Restifo, R. A., Farmer, T. A. 1962. "Spironolactone and gynecomastia." *Lancet* 2:1280.

Reyes, A. J., Olhaberry, J. V., Leary, W. P. 1983. "Urinary zinc excretion, diuretics, zinc deficiency and some side-effects of diuretics." *S Afr Med J* 64:936–41.

Rosenthal, J. et al. 1979. "Treatment of hypertension with a beta-adrenoceptor blocker: A multicentre trial with pindolol." *Br J Clin Pract* 33:165–81.

Ruedy, J., Davies, R. O. 1967. "A comparative clinical trial of guanoxan and guanethidine in essential hypertension." *Clin Pharmacol Ther* 8:38–47.

Scheingold, L. D., Wagner, N. N. 1974. *Sound sex and the aging heart,* p. 127. New York: Human Sciences Press.

Schimert, G., Buschbeck, K. 1981. "Multicentre study with nadolol in hypertension." In *International experience with nadolol,* edited by F. Gross, pp. 197–205. Proceedings Symposium, Squibb Europe Ltd. London: Academic Press.

Schinger, A., Gifford, R. W. 1962. "Guanethidine, a new antihypertensive agent: Experience in the treatment of 36 patients with severe hypertension." *Mayo Clin Proc* 37:100–08.

Schneider, J., Kaffarnik, H. 1975. "Impotence in patients with clofibrate." *Atherosclerosis* 21:455–57.

Seagraves, R. T., Madsen, R., Carter, C. S. et al. 1985. "Erectile dysfunction associated with pharmacological agents." In *Diagnosis and treatment of erectile disturbances,* edited by R. T. Seagraves and H. W. Schoenberg, pp. 23–63. New York: Plenum.

Semmens, J. P., Semmens, F. J. 1978. "Inadequate vaginal lubrication." *Med Asp Hum Sex* 12:58–71.

Schocket, B. R. 1976. "Medical aspects of sexual dysfunction." *Drug Ther* 6:37–42.

Slag, M. F., Morley, J. E., Elson, M. K. et al. 1983. "Impotence in medical clinic outpatients." *JAMA* 249:1736–40.

Smith, W. G. 1962. "Spironolactone and gynecomastia." *Lancet* 2:886.

Spark, R. F., Melby, J. C. 1968. "Aldosteronism in hypertension: The spironolactone response test." *Ann Intern Med* 69:685–91.

Sperzel, W. D., Glassman, H. N., Jordan, D. C. et al. 1986. "Overall safety of terazosin as an antihypertensive agent." *Amer J Med* 80:77–81.

Stessman, J., Ben-Ishay, D. 1980. "chlorthalidone-induced impotence." *Brit Med J* 281:714.

Stokes, G. S., Gain, J. M., Mahony, J. F. et al. 1977. "Long-term use of prazosin in combination or alone for treating hypertension." *Med J of Australia* (Spec. Suppl.) 2:13–16.

Stokes, G. S., Oates, H. F. 1978. "Prazosin, new alpha-adrenergic blocking agent in treatment of hypertension." *Cardiovasc Med* 3:41–57.

Stokes, J. F. 1962. "Unexpected gynecomastia." *Lancet* 2:911.

Story, N. L. 1974. "Sexual dysfunction resulting from drug side effects." *J Sex Res* 10:132–49.

Sussman, R. M. 1963. "Spironolactone and gynecomastia." *Lancet* 1:58.

Tanner, L. A., Bosco, L. A. 1988. "Gynecomastia associated with calcium channel blocker therapy." *Arch Intern Med* 148:379–80.

Tuchman, H., Crumpton, C. W. 1955. "A comparison of rauwolfia serpentina compound, crude root, alseroxylon derivative and single alkaloid in the treatment of hypertension." *Am Heart J* 49:742–50.

Turkington, R. W. 1972. "Prolactin secretion in patients treated with various drugs." *Arch Intern Med* 130:349–54.

Veterans Administration Cooperative Study Group on Antihypertensive Agents. 1981. "Comparison of prazosin with hydralazine in patients receiving hydrochlorothiazide." *Circulation* 64:772–79.

Wahl, B. N., Turlapaty, P., Singh, B. N. 1985. "Comparison of acebutolol and propranolol in essential hypertension." *Amer Heart J* 109:313–21.

Wallis, A. A., Bell, R., Sutherland, P. W. 1977. "Propranolol and Peyronie's disease." *Lancet* 2:980.

Warren, S. C., Warren, S. G. 1977. "Propranolol and sexual impotence." *Ann Int Med* 86:112.

Warren, S. G., Brewer, D. L., Orgain, E. S. 1976. "Long-term propranolol therapy for angina pectoris." *Am J Cardiol* 37:420–26.

Williams, E. 1962. "Spironolactone and gynecomastia." *Lancet* 2:1113.

Williams, G. H., Croog, S. H., Levine, S. et al. 1987. "Impact of antihypertensive therapy on quality of life: Effect of hydrochlorothiazide." *J of Hypertension* 5:S29–S35.

Yendt, E. R., Guay, G. F., Garcia, D. A. 1970. "The use of thiazides in the prevention of renal calculi." *Can Med Assoc J* 102:614–20.

Yudkin, J. S. 1977. "Peyronie's disease in association with metoprolol." *Lancet* 2:1355.

Zacharias, F. J. 1980. "Comparison of the side effects of different beta-blockers in the treatment of hypertension." *Primary Cardiol* 6:86–89.

Zacharias, F. J., Cowan, K. J., Cuthbertson, P. J. R. et al. 1977. "Atenolol in hypertension: A study of long-term therapy." *Postgraduate Med J* 53:102.

Zarren, H. S., Black, P. M. 1975. "Unilateral gynecomastia and impotence during low-dose spironolactone administration in men." *Milit Med* 140:417–19.

8
Sexual Counseling and Rehabilitation of the Cardiovascular Patient

Sexual counseling and rehabilitation should be a vital part of the overall rehabilitation of the cardiovascular patient. Sex is woven into the everyday life of many people and if the cardiovascular patient is to return to the optimal premorbid, physical, emotional and social status, and vocational and recreational activity, attention should be paid to his or her sexuality. For patients who were sexually active before the development of cardiovascular disease, a cardiovascular event, or surgery, return to sexual activity may have a significant positive impact on their psychological well-being, confidence in recovery and rehabilitation, emotional relationship with their spouse or partner, and overall quality of life.

THE QUALITY OF LIFE

The term "quality of life" integrates a wide range of capabilities, limitations, symptoms, and psychosocial characteristics that describe an individual's ability both to perform a variety of roles and derive satisfaction or enjoyment from doing so (Van Dam, Somers and Beck-Couzijn 1981). The health professional should consider the patients' perceptions of the significance or impact of the disease and its treatment on their ability to function in everyday life and their resultant sense of gratification and well-being (Wenger 1984). This incorporates the subjective component that reflects the patients' values, beliefs, and satisfactions as well as the priority or importance assigned to various roles. It may differ in subgroups of patients with varying severities and durations of disease and in populations whose culture and background assign different values to varied social roles, for example, job, recreation, family interactions, and participation in community life and civic activities.

Often the physician becomes preoccupied with the diagnostic and therapeutic aspects of the disease, ignoring the overall well-being and life satisfaction to which the patient is looking forward. Physicians are becoming aware that the major goal of therapy for most patients with chronic cardiovascular illness is not to cure the disease, but rather toimprove the quality of life. Patients would like to remain active, productive, and independent with few or none of the financial and emotional impacts of the illness. As we measure the course of a disease and the results of treatment, it is always important to remember that in addition to length, life has depth. The wise and compassionate physician includes in his or her calculations this second dimension (Eiseman 1981). Consideration of quality of life appears particularly useful when assessing the end points or outcome of treatment. This is encountered, for example, when deciding about the optimal clinical management, whether medical or surgical, of patients with angina pectoris, single or double vessel disease, or mild to moderate hypertension for whom a physiologic rather than pharmacologic regimen (with side effects on intellectual functioning and sexual performance) may be effective (Wenger 1984; Furberg 1984).

The quality of life has been more accurately described in terms of three major components: functional capacity perceptions, symptoms, and the consequences of symptoms (Najman and Levine 1981). The functional capacity has been defined as the patient's capability to carry out the usual activities of day to day life, such as self-care activities, social function, and intellectual and emotional function. The functional capacity also determines the resultant occupational and economic status of the patient. Family relationships and responsibilities and marital satisfaction form an additional element of functional capacity. It is important to take into consideration those aspects that the patient perceives as important to the quality of life. The patient's perceptions of general health status, life satisfaction, and happiness are entirely subjective assessments. The quality of life may also be affected by the symptoms of the disease and the degree of impairment. This may be reflected in alteration of activity in an attempt to limit the symptoms or in increased amounts of medications required to alleviate the symptoms, which may lead to side effects that may outweigh or substantially reduce the potential benefits of the therapeutic intervention. In a patient who is apparently well or minimally symptomatic and whose disease has a favorable outlook, even minimal or modest unfavorable alterations from medical management may be deemed unacceptable. On the other hand, in a patient who is chronically ill, whose disease carries a poor prognosis, and who has severe symptoms that limit function, modest improvements in functional performance, social relationships, and emotional satisfaction resulting from treatment can be considered to significantly improve the quality of life. Patients with chronic congestive heart failure are in this category. This final common pathway of many cardiovascular disorders is characterized by severe and progressive symptoms and dietary and activity restrictions and requires the administration of multiple medications. Because these patients are so seriously ill, virtually all components of quality of life may be influenced by an intervention. Examples of pertinent function include self-care and ambulatory ability, home management, the ability to engage in pleasurable activities — such as hobbies, recreational activities, and sexual activity — the performance of social roles with family and friends, and such other features of emotional status as expectations, mood, life satisfaction, and optimism about the future (Wenger 1984).

The expert clinician and people working with a patient, such as the rehabilitation nurse, a psychologist, a marital or sex counselor, should tailor a plan of care to meet the specific needs and expectations of the individual; the plan should be dictated by medical and also personal and social factors.

In order to adequately deal with issues related to a patient's quality of life, there must be effective communication between the patient and health professionals, especially the physician. However, for the physician who responds to the renewed emphasis on quality of life issues, recurrent dilemmas and traditional problems in medical practice may become more sharply focused (Levine and Croog 1984). While acknowledging the importance of quality of life concerns for the patients, many physicians differ in regard to the degree of emphasis that they can place on such matters in day-to-day clinical care. Some believe that if there is a large number of patients in the waiting room anticipating the application of special technical skills, they may not be well justified in spending time with individual patients to explore quality of life problems. Some indirect evidence from many empirical sources indicates general patterns of limited contact between physician and patient in the therapeutic process (Hauser 1981). According to data from the National Survey of Physician Practices, the time spent in face-to-face contact between physician and patient in an office visit has been reported as ten minutes or less in one-third of office visits of cardiac patients and between eleven and fifteen minutes in another one-third (U.S. Dept. of Health 1981). Some physicians believe that as professionals trained in scientific medicine they have to give priority to problems of physical conditioning and survival.

Dealing with quality of life concerns of patients is indeed likely to require more time. In a busy clinic or private office practice, resources and techniques may be developed to get information on patients' quality of life concerns. Questionnaires are being developed that can assist in rapid collection of key information and scores on these instruments can also serve as measures to document progress. Some of these questionnaires can be self-administered by patients and can serve both as sources of information on main issues and as guides for the physician to use in targeting problem areas to address (Levine and Croog 1984). Use of auxiliary personnel and referrals may be very useful in assuring that the quality of life concerns of the patient are addressed. Rehabilitation nurses, special rehabilitation programs, psychiatrists, psychologists, marital or sex counselors, social workers, clergy, and others may be of great assistance.

SEX EDUCATION

A major communication gap between the physician and the patient or his or her spouse involves the patient's sexual concerns (Papadopoulos 1978; Papadopoulos et al. 1980; Papadopoulos et al. 1983). Lack of training programs in sexuality in medical schools, inadequate information and literature on the sexual concerns and problems of the cardiovascular patient, and the physician's personal prejudices or difficulties in dealing with the subject probably play a role. Many physicians are often aware that some of the medical problems they see have sexual components, but they feel more comfortable ignoring than bringing them out in the open. Discomfort in dealing with sexuality is widespread and medical professionals are no exception. On the other hand, the members of the medical profession, because of their training and knowledge of anatomy and physiology, are assumed by the population at large to be experts on sexuality.

According to Lief (1974), sexual education constituted a glaring gap in professional preparation in medical schools. In 1963 only three schools had such material formally in their curricula. By 1969 there were 43 medical schools having some organized instruction in sex. Currently, most schools provide some material on sexuality, but the course content varies from a few lectures to full-fledged mandatory courses and electives. Sex education for medical students should cover three major areas: knowledge, making it possible for the doctor to deal with the patient's questions and myths; attitudes, since only a doctor comfortable with his or her own sexuality can deal comfortably with the patient's sexual problems; skills, so that the doctor can take efficient sexual histories and act on them effectively. Formal lectures and small group discussions complemented by the appropriate audio-visual aids may provide the necessary clinical information, but the students should also actually see and counsel patients with close supervision and direction by a faculty member.

Medical students bring to medical school the same misconceptions, misinformation, and anxieties regarding sex that any other group of similarly educated people have. According to Labby (1983), programs in human sexuality currently offered in most medical schools may not have the expected impact. Medical students are often interested in sexual education primarily for personal reasons. After they become physicians, they do not easily take on the responsibility when the need of counseling patients regarding sexuality and sexual function arises.

SEXUAL COUNSELING

Often the physician waits until the patient broaches the subject of sexual matters. In our studies based on interviews with patients, 11 percent of the physicians raised the topic of sexual activity after myocardial infarction in the early 1970s and 18 percent in the late 1970s (Papadopoulos 1978; Papadopoulos et al. 1983). This is in contrast to a survey of physicians (Wenger et al. 1982) which reported that a high percentage of them provide routine in-hospital counseling and education of patients about diet, smoking, return to work, and resumption of sexual activity. This raises the question as to how thorough and comprehensive the latter instructions are and whether they address the specific concerns and problems of the patient and spouse.

Physicians must assume the responsibility of carefully addressing the topic of sexuality since they are in an excellent position to help those distressed by marital and sexual difficulties. There is considerable information on the favorable outcome of therapy for psychologic and organic sexual problems (Kolodny, Masters and Johnson 1979; Montague et al. 1979; Kaplan 1980; Osborne 1981; Federman 1982).

It is important for the physician to take a sexual history along with the medical history. Recent studies (Slag et al. 1983; Lanier and Graveson 1982) stated that medical practitioners often neglect the sexual history. Yet it should be considered part of the routine data base. A recent study showed that patients seen by primary care internists frequently have sexual problems and that when the sexual history is included as part of the medical data base, both patients and physicians regard it as beneficial (Ende, Rockwell and Glasgow 1984). Two hundred twenty-eight patients, regardless of whether their physician had discussed sex, were asked if they believed such a discussion was or would have been appropriate. Ninety-one percent answered "yes" and 9 percent answered "no." Among the patients whose physicians had taken a sexual history, the approval was almost unanimous (98 percent). In contrast, among those patients whose physicians had failed to include the sexual history in the interview, 78 percent indicated that it would have been appropriate. Sexual problems and concerns were found to be widespread. In this study, the physicians could not predict from demographic characteristics which patients will have a positive sexual history.

Sexuality is a personal and sensitive area and taking a sexual history is not always easy or simple, but it must be part of a complete medical evaluation. Denslow Lewis, in addressing the Annual Meeting of the American Medical Association 90 years ago, urged his colleagues to consider their patients' sexual health. "It is, therefore, proper," he said, "for medical men in their deliberations to take cognizance of this factor in human life. They should know its relationship to health and happiness. They should not be deterred from its scientific investigation by false modesty or by fear of being accused of sensationalism" (Lewis 1983).

The patient's ease and ability in discussing his or her sexual problems vary directly with the physician's ability and confidence in dealing with the situation. A physician who feels comfortable in dealing with this topic can impart some of this attitude to the normally embarrassed patient. Patients ordinarily expect that physicians will use adequate medical terms, even if they must explain some words. This is a matter of creating confidence by approaching the problem scientifically and with dignity (Klemer 1966). The successful physician is one who is warm and understanding, who knows himself or herself and who is competent and believes that he or she can help the patient. It is very useful to discuss sexual problems with the patient and thereafter, in the presence of the spouse or partner. The couple's sex life should be dealt with in the context of their relationship. Spouses often have concerns and problems in regard to their marital status and sexual relations. Often their sexual and affectional needs are frustrated. The couple's desire for sexual attention and pleasure and for affection often do not coincide. The patient and spouse will feel comfortable in openly communicating with the physician or other counselor when they can sense his or her genuine interest and desire to help them. At times, they will want to delve deeper into the sexual aspects of their problems than the counselor had planned.

Often a patient will find it extremely difficult to talk about sex. In this case, the health professional should double efforts to provide a warm and secure atmosphere in which the patient may better express himself or herself. The counselor should be a very patient and reassuring listener, responding in a careful and thoughtful way. It will be necessary in some cases to directly help the inhibited patient, perhaps by giving some pertinent information followed by a deliberate oblique question (Klemer 1966). Attention should be paid to the psychological and not just the technical aspects of sexual activity.

At times advice given to patients is more related to the physician's own sexual practices than to sound physiological data or to the patient's needs and physical capability. A physician with conflicts and inhibitions in his or her own sexual life may, for example, prescribe an exceedingly long period of sexual abstinence for the post-myocardial infarction patient who may have been sexually active before, oblivious to the fact that this may induce stress and marital difficulties. On the other hand, a physician who is enjoying frequent sexual activity may advise the patient to go to the other extreme.

Sometimes the patient may present with a host of physical complaints induced by psychological stress from various sexual problems. He or she may have palpitations, excessive sweating, fainting spells, hyperventilation, neurodermatitis, and so forth. In such instances, the physician's lack of factual knowledge and comfort with the area of sexuality may lead to inappropriate medical interpretation. Furthermore, to be able to establish a therapeutic dialogue with his or her patients, the physician should be knowledgeable and sensitive to social class and culturally-determined differences in sexual attitudes, values, and practices.

Similarly, nurses who may have to deal with the topic of human sexuality in their nursing practices should first accept and feel comfortable with their own sexuality and have acquired the knowledge and developed an interest in this topic. They have to be able to resolve their feelings about patients whose sexual orientation or practices are different from their own, because sex is an intimate part of a person's life. The special rapport a nurse can establish with a patient gives him or her a definite advantage in incorporating sexual counseling into nursing practice. Patients feel a closeness to nurses because of the intimacy necessary in providing nursing care. In interviews with patients or patients' spouses, the nurses were frequently mentioned, together with the physicians, as the most desirable professionals to provide sexual counseling after heart attacks (Papadopoulos et al. 1980; Papadopoulos et al. 1983). When nurses and doctors work well together, they can make an excellent team.

In discussing problems dealing with sexuality and, especially the sexual concerns and problems of the cardiovascular patient, it is vital to be acquainted with the available information and literature. All professionals who may have to provide sexual counseling to cardiovascular patients should be acquainted with the particular physiopathological, pharmacological, and emotional aspects of their disease. Furthermore, the counselor who knows the usual sexual difficulties and problems of these patients may reassure and appropriately guide and help them. For beneficial physician-patient communication, the physician should be sure that the patient understands the sexual physiology and behavior relevant to the case. Even patients who know a great deal about sex structure and function may be missing the one vital piece of information that is crucial to their sexual adjustment.

Providing available printed material in regard to sexual activity after a cardiovascular event, especially a heart attack, should be supplemented with further explanation and question answering by the physician or rehabilitation nurse to assure comprehension and avoid misinterpretations.

When necessary, the physician should not hesitate to refer the patient to a sex counselor or a psychotherapist, although occasionally the physician is the only counseling resource available. The counselor may help communication between the marriage partners and this can help sexual rehabilitation and resumption of sexual activity (Papadopoulos et al. 1980).

Clinical experiences suggest that after an acute illness many patients and their spouses make a satisfactory sexual adjustment without outside help. Others, however, deal with the problem of sexual needs in a painful and awkward way, if they are able to face the problem at all (Ford and Orfirer 1967). This difficulty comes at a time when the couple is least prepared for more strain on an already heavily burdened relationship. The patient often has a seriously damaged self-image and the anxiety and sense of loss may lead to a dependent and helpless state. In the hospital, the patient may seek self-reassurance. Some patients after a myocardial infarction may make remarks with sexual overtones, or a hemiplegic patient may, unnecessarily, expose himself to female nurses and attendants.

Sexual concerns and anxiety should be addressed early and sexual counseling should be part of early rehabilitation, starting before and continuing after discharge from the hospital. The patient has to adapt emotionally to his or her handicap and the family must be prepared for adaptation. A sympathetic and attentive physician or nurse may help the patient express his or her concerns and alleviate any fears. No health professional should assume that every person who has suffered a physical impairment would have withdrawn emotional attention from ordinary interests and sexuality.

In some cases, the physician has to deal with aspects of sexuality after a cardiovascular event. In other cases, however, this topic can be addressed earlier, such as before cardiac or vascular surgery. In general, patients who have had good sexual adjustment ask about sexual activity in advance of the surgery because they do want to continue it. When a patient does not raise the question, it may be because of shyness or discomfort with approaching this topic or because he or she has been sexually inactive or because the couple never had good sexual adjustment. Therefore the physician or rehabilitation nurse should approach the subject in a sensitive and positive way.

Some health professionals have difficulty viewing older people as sexual beings and may completely neglect the sexual concerns of older patients. That sexual desire and expression are normal in the elderly is commonly appreciated today, but it is often not translated into clinical practice. Perhaps a discussion with the patient on the subject of sex is imagined to be mutually uncomfortable, not worth the time of a busy practitioner, or something that simply is not done with patients older than the physician (Glover 1977). Physicians may use a practical approach in dealing with this sensitive subject with the elderly: promoting discussion, listening in a sympathetic non-judgmental way, and offering compassionate advice. Many elderly patients, despite first denials, do want to talk about their sexual problems. In fact, they welcome discussion. Glover (1977) found he is telling such patients what they know intuitively but want affirmed: As people age, the intimacy of the sex act, the sharing, closeness and caressing have a meaning and pleasure that may be exquisitely real, whereas achievement of orgasm is largely symbolic. Just lying in another person's arms may bring greater satisfaction in old age than in youth. The elderly patient may be highly receptive to those observations, as affirmation of his or her normality. The physician should also keep in mind that one woman in four over the age of 70 masturbates, and it may be the only outlet for the woman who has no male partner (Glover 1977). Understanding the overall physiological changes in the sexuality of the elderly will provide more effective sexual counseling of the cardiovascular patient.

Adherence to the following guidelines for sexual counseling will determine its effectiveness (Cohen 1986):

1. Maintain a non-judgmental attitude. Such an attitude by the counselor is absolutely essential. The patient's mores or sexual preferences are not the concern of the counselor.
2. Identify from behavioral cues when the patient is ready to discuss sexual concerns. Statements like, "I wonder if I'll ever be whole again?" "When can I get back to my usual activity?" "How is all this going to affect my life?" can all indicate a need for sexual counseling.
3. Keep the issue of sexuality in perspective for the patient and spouse. The topic of sexuality should be placed in the context of other problems.
4. Provide a conducive environment for counseling. Counseling should be done in private. Separate counseling sessions for patient and partner often permit the easy and open discussion of worries and feelings. Joint counseling of both the patient and partner can be done prior to discharge.
5. Seek feedback to determine if counseling has been effective. Factors that affect the amount of information the patient retains include the patient's readiness to learn, the type of material and presentation, the significance of the material to the patient, the climate of the learning situation, and the patient's stage of illness.

REHABILITATION

Sexual rehabilitation is an element of the overall rehabilitation of the cardiovascular patient. Improvement in the physical, psychological, and vocational aspects of rehabilitation will have a positive impact on sexual activity. Any comprehensive rehabilitation program should include functional evaluation, exercise training, patient and family education, as well as psychosocial, sexual, and vocational counseling. Physical exercise programs are essential for the post-myocardial infarction patient, post-coronary bypass surgery patient, the stroke victim, and the patient with vascular disease. A rehabilitation program should strive to initiate intervention and counseling as early as medically possible during the hospitalization. A cardiologist, a rehabilitation nurse, an exercise physiologist, and a physical therapist are often involved in evaluating the functional capacity of the patient and defining the type, intensity, and frequency of exercise programs for rehabilitation. Whenever cardiac instability is anticipated during exercise programs, cardiac monitoring should be implemented during the sessions. The programs should be individualized and the training and beneficial effects periodically measured. The major beneficial effects of exercise for patients with angina, or post-myocardial infarction or post-coronary bypass surgery lead to improvement in functional capacity. They include:

1. increased maximal cardiac output and oxygen consumption,
2. decreased resting heart rate,
3. lesser increase in heart rate and systolic blood pressure for any level of work,
4. more rapid return to normal of the exercise heart rate,
5. decreased or absent angina pectoris at work loads that previously induced angina, and
6. decreased or absent ST-T electrocardiographic ischemic changes at work loads that previously induced them.

In the case of the stroke or peripheral vascular disease patient, the aim is a more independent, self-reliant, and more freely ambulating individual. Improvement in functional capacity, control of symptoms related to exertion, and improvement of mobility have a positive effect on sexual activity and enjoyment by improving self-esteem and confidence and increasing exercise tolerance.

Vocational concerns particularly affect the younger patients, who fear for their job and the family's economic future. Evidence of potential disability before returning to work should be analyzed to determine whether it is due to psychological or physiological problems, or both. The attitude of the physician in actively encouraging prompt return to work appears to be a significant factor. Unfortunately, individuals who do the more physically demanding work are often patients with limited educational skills, and this does not allow much opportunity for job change. Vocational rehabilitation agencies may be valuable for such patients in providing employment counseling and job retraining. However, such other factors as management and labor attitudes and practices, insurance and compensation regulations, legal considerations, and so forth may determine the vocational success of cardiovascular patients. For the patient who is ambitious and eager or needs to return to work, failure of re-employment may lead to psychological problems with a negative impact on his or her self-image and psychological and sexual health (Wenger 1981).

Psychological problems are common in patients with cardiovascular diseases. Most people who have experienced cardiovascular surgery or myocardial infarction or who cope with cardiovascular illness on a continuing basis experience some degree of anxiety. Others may develop associated depressive symptoms. They may have feelings of worthlessness, guilt, helplessness, hopelessness, sadness, and loss of interest in work and sexual activity.

Patients with cardiovascular diseases face, or are victims of, frightening life events and invalidism, stroke, or death (Freeman 1983). The anxiety, with or without depressive symptoms, and depression belie the patient's painful vision of a dismal future with loss of independence, strength, and energy; reduced earning power; demands to abandon pleasant habits; restrictions on activities; sexual problems; incapacitation; and premature aging. A myocardial infarction in particular has a profound impact on self-image, attitudes, and expectations. Life seems to be sharply delineated into the "before" and "after" periods of the patient's illness (Wolff 1964). A study of psychosocial outcome in patients undergoing open heart surgery (Heller et al. 1974) found that in spite of little physical impairment, patients became less self-reliant and more socially constricted with decreased expression of sexual and aggressive drives. One year after the operation, one-third were still encountering significant psychologic hindrance to recovery, with considerable anxiety, depression, somatic preoccupation, social withdrawal, and impaired sexual function.

Depression and anxiety normally run their course and improve with time. Those who attend rehabilitation programs seem to recover more completely. Exercise decreases tension and depression, while improving self-esteem in subjects who comply with training programs. The specific aspects of exercise that produce psychologic benefits have not been determined but may include social participation, sense of mastering and achievement, and expectation of improvement (Goff and Dimsdale 1985). In certain cases the use of anti-anxiety or antidepressant medications may be needed. In such cases the improvement of the psychological status of the patient may improve the lack of libido or other sexual difficulties. On the other hand, the negative sexual side effects that these medications may at times cause should be kept in mind.

A spouse plays a major role in the patient's re-adjustment during convalescence and in the rate and extent of the patient's rehabilitation and psychologic recovery (Skelton and Dominian 1974). There is also a definite correlation between the emotional relationship of the couple and the resumption of sexual activity (Papadopoulos et al. 1983).

In the absence of a spouse, a patient who has a warm extended family or some close friends for company can compensate for a close relationship like marriage. It is important for the physician, the rehabilitation nurse, or the social worker to encourage these interactions and to return the patient to a social environment with which he or she is acquainted.

Formal family counseling is often necessary to provide an integrated program of emotional support, education, and physical activity as well as a forum in which to resolve fears and misconceptions and permit the definition of roles within the family.

In conclusion, the health professional should reassure the patient that there is life after development of cardiovascular disease, a cardiovascular event or surgery and, at the same time, realize that for most patients it is not only the length of life that counts but its depth and quality, and that sex is part of it.

BIBLIOGRAPHY

Cohen, A. J. 1986. "Sexual counseling of the patient following myocardial infarction." *Crit Care Nurse* 6:18–26.

Eiseman, B. 1981. "The second dimension." *Arch Surg* 116:11–13.

Ende, J., Rockwell, S., Glasgow, M. 1984. "The sexual history in general medicine practice." *Arch Intern Med* 144:558–61.

Federman, D. 1982. "Impotence: Etiology and management." *Hosp Pract* 17: 155–59.

Ford, A. B., Orfirer, A. P. 1967. "Sexual behavior and the chronically ill patient." *Med Asp of Hum Sex* 1:51–61.

Freeman, A. M. 1983. *Anxiety and anxiety with depressive symptoms in the patient with cardiac disorders*. Chicago: Pragmaton Publications.

Furberg, C. D. 1984. "The implications of treatment for quality of life." *Quality of Life and Cardiovascular Care* 1:37–39.

Glover, B. H. 1977. "Sex counseling of the elderly." *Hosp Pract* 12:101–13.

Goff, D., Dimsdale, J. E. 1985. "The psychologic effects of exercise." *J Cardiopulmonary Rehab* 5:234–40.

Hauser, S. T. 1981. "Physician-patient relationships." In *Social Contexts of Health Illness and Patient Care*, edited by E. Mishler, L. R. Amarasingham, S. T. Hauser et al. Cambridge: Cambridge University Press.

Heller, S., Frank, K., Kornfield, D. et al. 1974. "Psychological outcome following open heart surgery." *Arch Intern Med* 134:908–14.

Kaplan, H. S. 1980. "Sexual medicine: A progress report." *Arch Intern Med* 140:1575–76.

Klemer, R. H. 1966. "Talking with patients about sexual problems." *Postgraduate Med J* 40:160–66.

Kolodny, R. C., Master, W. H., Johnson, V. E. 1979. *Textbook of Sexual Medicine*. Boston: Little, Brown & Co.

Labby, D. H. 1983. "Iatrogenic effects on sexual function." *Med Asp of Hum Sex* 17:170–78.

Lanier, D. C., Graveson, R. G. 1982. "Detection of sexual problems by family medicine residents: Effect of a sex education program." *J Sex Educ Ther* 8:21–24.

Levine S., Croog, S. H. 1984. "The primary care physician and the patient's quality of life." *Quality of Life and Cardiovascular Care* 1:29–36.

Lewis, D. 1983. "The gynecologic consideration of the sexual act." *JAMA* 250:222–27.

Lief, H. I. 1974. "Sexual knowledge, attitudes and behavior of medical students: Implications for medical practice." In *Marital and Sexual Counseling in Medical Practice,* edited by D. W. Abse, N. E. Miller, L. Lois, pp. 447–94. Hagerstown: Harper & Row.

Montague, D. K., James, R. E., DeWolf, V. G. et al. 1979. "Diagnostic evaluation, classification and treatment of men with sexual dysfunction." *Urology* 14:545–548.

Najman, J. M., Levine, S. 1981. "Evaluating the impact of medical care and technologies on the quality of life: A review and critique." *Soc Sci Med* 15F:107–15.

Osborne, D. 1981. "Psychological aspects of male sexual dysfunction: Diagnosis and management." *Urology Clin North Am* 8:135–42.

Papadopoulos, C. 1978. "A survey of sexual activity after myocardial infarction." *Cardiovasc Med* 3:821–26.

Papadopoulos, C., Beaumont, C., Shelley, S. I. et al. 1983. "Myocardial infarction and sexual activity of the female patient." *Arch Intern Med* 143:1528–30.

Papadopoulos, C., Larrimore, P., Cardin, S. et al. 1980. "Sexual concerns and needs of the postcoronary patient's wife." *Arch Intern Med* 140:38–41.

Skelton, M., Dominian, J. 1974. "Psychological stress in wives of patients with myocardial infarction." In *Marital and sexual counseling in medical practice,* edited by D. W. Abse, N. E. Miller, L. Lois, pp. 259–65. Hagerstown: Harper & Row.

Slag, M. F., Morley, J. E., Elson, M. K. et al. 1983. "Impotence in medical clinic outpatients." *JAMA* 249:1736–40.

U.S. Department of Health, Education and Welfare. 1981. *Health,* p. 284. Publication No. (P.H.S.) 78-1232. Hyattsville, Md.: Public Health Service.

Van Dam, F. S. A. M., Somers, R., van Beck-Couzijn, A. L. 1981. "Quality of life: Some theoretical issues." *J Clin Pharmacol* 21:166S–68S.

Wenger, N. K. 1981. "Rehabilitation of the patient with symptomatic coronary atherosclerotic heart disease." Dallas: American Heart Association.

———. 1984. "The concept of quality of life: An appropriate consideration in clinical decision making affecting patients with cardiovascular disease." *Quality of Life and Cardiovascular Care* 1:8–13.

Wenger, N. K., Hellerstein, H. K., Blackburn, H. et al. 1982. "Physician practice in the management of patients with uncomplicated myocardial infarction: Changes in the past decade." *Circulation* 65:421–27.

Wolff, I. 1964. "Myocardial infarction: The experience." *Am J Nurs* 64:C4–9.

Index

About the Author

CHRIS PAPADOPOULOS is currently Chief of Cardiology at Harbor Hospital Center and Clinical Associate Professor of Medicine at the University of Maryland School of Medicine. A Diplomate of the American Board of Internal Medicine and the Board of Cardiovascular Disease, he is also Fellow of the American College of Physicians, the American College of Cardiology, the American College of Chest Physicians, and the Council of Clinical Cardiology of the American Heart Association. He is a member of the American Association of Cardiovascular and Pulmonary Rehabilitation, of the Council on Rehabilitation of the International Society and Federation of Cardiology and past president of the American Heart Association — Maryland Affiliate.

Dr. Papadopoulos has been interested in the sexual aspects of cardiac rehabilitation for many years and has presented numerous papers at national and international meetings. He is a member of the American Medical Writers Association and consulting editor of *Medical Aspects of Human Sexuality*. He has authored several articles on medical topics, including cardiology and medical aspects of human sexuality.